I0011260

Rust for the Brave

Build Ultra-Fast, Memory-Safe Applications with Confidence

Booker Blunt

Rafael Sanders

Miguel Farmer

Boozman Richard

All rights reserved

No part of this book may be reproduced, distributed, or transmitted in any form or by any means without the prior written permission of the publisher, except in the case of brief quotations embodied in critical reviews and certain other noncommercial uses permitted by right law.

How to Scan a Barcode to Get a Repository

1. **Install a QR/Barcode Scanner** – Ensure you have a barcode or QR code scanner app installed on your smartphone or use a built-in scanner in **GitHub, GitLab, or Bitbucket.**

2. **Open the Scanner** – Launch the scanner app and grant necessary camera permissions.

3. **Scan the Barcode** – Align the barcode within the scanning frame. The scanner will automatically detect and process it.

4. **Follow the Link** – The scanned result will display a **URL to the repository**. Tap the link to open it in your web browser or Git client.

5. **Clone the Repository** – Use **Git clone** with the provided URL to download the repository to your local machine.

Chapter 1: Getting Started with Rust

Introduction to Rust: Why Rust is Gaining Popularity in Systems Programming and Beyond

Rust is rapidly gaining traction as one of the most sought-after programming languages in the tech industry, and its rise to prominence is no accident. Its unique combination of performance, safety, and concurrency has made it the go-to language for system-level programming. If you've worked with languages like C or C++, you're probably familiar with the need to balance performance with the risk of memory errors. Rust solves this dilemma by offering low-level control over hardware and system resources while guaranteeing memory safety without a garbage collector. This is a huge benefit for developers who need to write reliable, efficient code for performance-critical applications.

One of the main reasons Rust is getting such widespread adoption is due to its strong emphasis on memory safety. In most programming languages, memory management is either handled by the developer (as in C/C++) or by a garbage collector (as in languages like Java and Python). However, both approaches come with their own set of issues—manual memory management often leads to bugs like dangling pointers or buffer overflows, while garbage collection can introduce unpredictable latency. Rust takes a different approach by enforcing strict rules on memory ownership and borrowing at compile-time, which eliminates many of these issues without sacrificing performance.

Rust is not just for systems programming anymore. Its use is expanding into various domains, including web development, game development, networking, and even embedded systems. As the software industry continues to evolve, Rust's ability to enable developers to build fast, safe, and concurrent applications is allowing it to become a general-purpose programming language of choice.

Setting Up the Environment: Installation of Rust, Setting Up the Rust Toolchain, and Configuring the Development Environment

Before diving into the language, the first step is to set up your development environment. Rust's installation process is straightforward and well-documented, and it involves a few steps that will get you up and running quickly.

To install Rust, head over to the official Rust website at https://rust-lang.org, where you can download the installation tool, `rustup`. `rustup` is the official installer and version management tool for Rust, and it will set up the Rust toolchain, which includes the Rust compiler (`rustc`), the package manager (`cargo`), and the standard library.

Once you've installed `rustup`, you'll need to configure your system's environment variables so that your terminal can recognize the Rust commands. This setup is typically done automatically, but on some systems, you may need to manually add Rust to your system's `PATH` variable. The `rustup` installer will also install the latest stable version of Rust, which is the recommended version for most users. Rust's versioning system ensures that you're always working with a reliable and stable build, and `rustup` also allows you to easily switch between different versions or toolchains as needed.

Once the installation is complete, you can verify that Rust has been properly installed by running the following command in your terminal:

```bash
rustc --version
```

This command will output the current version of the Rust compiler. You should see something like:

```scss
rustc 1.58.0 (7e3e9baf3 2022-01-04)
```

If you see this message, congratulations! Your Rust environment is set up and ready to go.

Rust Syntax Fundamentals: Basic Syntax, Variables, and Constants

Rust has a clean and modern syntax, but there are a few concepts that are essential to understand as you start writing Rust code. Let's begin by looking at how to define variables and constants.

In Rust, variables are immutable by default. This means that once a variable is assigned a value, you cannot change it unless you explicitly make it mutable. This is one of the ways Rust ensures memory safety and prevents unintended side effects in your code.

Here's a simple example of an immutable variable:

```rust
let x = 5;
```

In this case, x is a variable that holds the value 5. Since Rust variables are immutable by default, attempting to change the value of x later in the program would result in a compiler error. To make a variable mutable, you must use the `mut` keyword:

```rust
let mut x = 5;
x = 10;
```

Now, x is mutable, and you can change its value after it has been assigned.

Constants in Rust are similar to variables, but they are always immutable and are defined using the `const` keyword. Constants must also have their type explicitly specified:

```rust
rust
```

```rust
const MAX_POINTS: u32 = 100_000;
```

In this case, `MAX_POINTS` is a constant that holds the value `100,000`. The `u32` specifies that `MAX_POINTS` is an unsigned 32-bit integer. Constants are always in uppercase by convention.

Another important feature of Rust's syntax is its emphasis on type safety. When you declare a variable, you don't need to specify its type explicitly unless Rust cannot infer it. Rust has powerful type inference capabilities, which makes the syntax simple while still ensuring that the types of variables are correct.

For example:

```rust
rust
```

```rust
let x = 5; // Rust infers that x is an integer
let y: f64 = 3.14; // You can specify the type
explicitly
```

Hello, World!: Writing Your First Rust Program and Understanding the Output

Now that we've set up the environment and have a basic understanding of variables and constants, let's write our first Rust program: a simple "Hello, World!" application. This will give us a feel for Rust's syntax and how to compile and run programs.

Here's the code for a basic "Hello, World!" program in Rust:

rust

```rust
fn main() {
    println!("Hello, World!");
}
```

Let's break down the code:

1. `fn main()` defines the main function, which is the entry point for every Rust program.
2. The `println!` macro prints text to the console. Rust uses macros with an exclamation mark (`!`) at the end of their names to distinguish them from regular functions. In this case, `println!` prints the string `"Hello, World!"` to the screen.
3. The curly braces `{}` are used to denote the block of code that belongs to the `main` function.

To run this program, save it in a file called `main.rs`. Then, from the command line, navigate to the folder where you saved the file and run the following command:

```bash
bash
```

```
cargo run
```

This command compiles and runs the program. You should see the following output:

```
Hello, World!
```

Congratulations! You've just written and run your first Rust program.

Hands-on Project: A Simple "Hello, World!" Program, Followed by a Basic Calculator Application

Now that you have written your first program, let's build something a little more interactive. We'll create a simple calculator that can add, subtract, multiply, and divide two numbers.

Here's the code for our basic calculator:

```rust
rust

use std::io;

fn main() {
    println!("Enter the first number:");
```

```
    let mut num1 = String::new();
    io::stdin().read_line(&mut num1).expect("Failed
to read line");
    let num1: f64 =
num1.trim().parse().expect("Please enter a valid
number");

    println!("Enter the second number:");
    let mut num2 = String::new();
    io::stdin().read_line(&mut num2).expect("Failed
to read line");
    let num2: f64 =
num2.trim().parse().expect("Please enter a valid
number");

    println!("Enter an operation (+, -, *, /):");
    let mut operation = String::new();
    io::stdin().read_line(&mut
operation).expect("Failed to read line");
    let operation = operation.trim();

    let result = match operation {
        "+" => num1 + num2,
        "-" => num1 - num2,
        "*" => num1 * num2,
        "/" => num1 / num2,
        _ => {
            println!("Invalid operation");
            return;
```

```
        }
    };

    println!("The result is: {}", result);
}
```

In this calculator program, we:

1. Prompt the user to input two numbers.
2. Parse the user input from a string to a `f64` (floating-point number).
3. Ask the user to choose an operation (+, -, *, /).
4. Perform the operation using a `match` expression, which selects the appropriate operation based on the user's input.
5. Display the result of the operation.

Once again, you can run the program using `cargo run`, and it will prompt you to enter numbers and select an operation. For example:

```sql
Enter the first number:
5
Enter the second number:
10
Enter an operation (+, -, *, /):
+
The result is: 15
```

By completing this hands-on project, you've not only written your first Rust program but also created a more interactive program that performs real calculations. This is a great starting point for your journey into Rust, and you'll build upon these basic concepts as you continue to explore the language.

Chapter 2: Understanding Rust's Ownership Model

Memory Management Basics: Explaining Ownership, Borrowing, and Lifetimes

When it comes to systems programming, one of the biggest challenges has always been managing memory efficiently and safely. Languages like C and C++ give developers direct control over memory, but that comes at the price of potential errors, such as null pointer dereferencing and memory leaks. Rust, on the other hand, approaches memory management differently. Through its unique ownership model, Rust provides both speed and safety without a garbage collector.

At the core of Rust's memory management system is a set of rules for ownership, borrowing, and lifetimes. These rules ensure that every piece of memory in a program is either owned by one variable or borrowed by others, making sure there are no data races, memory leaks, or invalid references.

The ownership model is designed around three primary principles:

1. **Ownership**: Every value in Rust has a variable that is its owner. A value can only have one owner at a time. Once ownership is transferred to another variable, the original variable can no longer access the value. This guarantees that no two variables can inadvertently modify the same piece of memory.

2. **Borrowing**: Instead of transferring ownership, Rust allows variables to borrow references to data. Borrowing comes in two flavors: immutable and mutable. A borrow is temporary, and the borrowing rules ensure that no data is modified unexpectedly while it's being borrowed.

3. **Lifetimes**: In addition to ownership and borrowing, Rust uses lifetimes to track how long references are valid. The lifetime system ensures that references do not outlive the data they point to, preventing issues like dangling pointers.

This model may seem strict at first, but it's designed to enforce memory safety without runtime overhead. By making these rules part of the language's core, Rust is able to provide guarantees that are typically only available at runtime in other languages, such as safe memory access and preventing invalid references.

The Borrowing Rules: Immutable vs. Mutable References

In Rust, borrowing means allowing another part of your program to access a value without taking ownership of it. Borrowing is Rust's way of ensuring that multiple parts of your program can access data without conflicting with one another, all while maintaining safety. There are two kinds of borrowing: immutable borrowing and mutable borrowing.

1. **Immutable References**:
   - With immutable references, you are allowed to read the data but not modify it. Multiple immutable references can exist simultaneously, as long as no mutable references exist at the same time. This is because reading data from multiple sources doesn't pose any risk of corruption.
   - For example:

   rust

   ```
   let x = 5;
   let y = &x; // immutable borrow
   let z = &x; // another immutable borrow
   println!("x: {}, y: {}", x, y);
   ```

- o The key takeaway here is that multiple parts of your program can safely read from the same data without any conflicts.

2. **Mutable References**:
   - o A mutable reference allows you to modify the data it points to. However, Rust enforces a rule that there can only be **one mutable reference** to a piece of data at any given time. This rule prevents data races where two parts of the program try to change the same value at once.
   - o For example:

```rust
let mut x = 5;
let y = &mut x; // mutable borrow
*y += 1; // modifying the data through
the reference
println!("x: {}", x); // prints 6
```

   - o In this case, Rust ensures that no other part of the program can borrow x while it is being mutated. If you try to create more than one mutable reference, the compiler will throw an error.

Rust enforces these rules at compile time, which means that by the time your code runs, the Rust compiler has already verified that no data races or invalid accesses can occur.

Why Rust is Memory-Safe: Preventing Null Pointers and Dangling References

One of the main problems that Rust's ownership model solves is the issue of memory safety. In many programming languages, such as C and C++, developers are responsible for manually managing memory. This often leads to issues like **null pointer dereferencing** and **dangling references**—where a program attempts to access memory that's either invalid or has already been freed.

Rust prevents these issues with its ownership and borrowing model:

1. **Null Pointers**: In languages like C, null pointers are a common source of bugs. Rust takes a different approach by eliminating the concept of null pointers altogether. Instead of using null to represent an invalid reference, Rust uses the `Option` type, which explicitly handles the possibility of an absent value.
   - For example:

     ```rust
     ```

```
let x: Option<i32> = Some(5);   // x
contains a value
let y: Option<i32> = None;      // y is an
empty value
```

- o   With the `Option` type, Rust forces developers to explicitly handle the case where a value might be absent, preventing the typical runtime null reference errors.

2. **Dangling References**: A dangling reference occurs when a reference points to memory that has been deallocated. In languages like C, this can lead to undefined behavior. Rust prevents dangling references through its strict lifetime rules. The compiler tracks how long a reference is valid and ensures that it doesn't outlive the data it points to. If you try to use a reference after the data it points to has been deallocated, the compiler will prevent the code from compiling.

- o   For example:

```rust
let s;
{
    let x = String::from("Hello");
    s = &x;   // s borrows x, but x goes
out of scope
```

```
}
// Here, s would be a dangling reference
and the code will not compile.
```

o   The Rust compiler catches this error at compile-time,
ensuring that no part of your program can access
data that no longer exists.

With these guarantees, Rust ensures that programs cannot
accidentally introduce bugs related to invalid memory access, such
as null pointer dereferencing or using dangling references. The
borrow checker and the ownership system are there to enforce that
all memory accesses are safe, with no runtime overhead.

Hands-on Project: Building a Function that Manages Data Ownership Between Different Scopes

Let's put what we've learned into practice by building a function that
handles data ownership between different scopes. We'll create a
simple example that demonstrates ownership, borrowing, and
mutable references.

Here's a simple program that simulates a scenario where ownership
is transferred between functions, and borrowing is used to allow
multiple parts of the program to access the same data:

```rust
rust

fn main() {
    let s1 = String::from("Hello, Rust!");   // s1
owns the string

    // Ownership of the string is transferred to s2
    let s2 = take_ownership(s1);

    // We can no longer use s1 here, as its ownership
has been moved

    // Borrowing s2 to print its value
    print_string(&s2);   // Immutable borrow

    // Now we can create a mutable reference to s2
    let mut s3 = s2;
    change_string(&mut s3); // Mutable borrow

    // Print the modified string
    println!("Modified string: {}", s3);
}

fn take_ownership(s: String) -> String {
    println!("Inside take_ownership: {}", s);
    s  // ownership of s is returned here
}

fn print_string(s: &String) {
```

```
    println!("Inside print string: {}", s);   //
Immutable borrow
}


fn change_string(s: &mut String) {
    s.push_str(" Now we are changing it!");
}
```

What's Happening in the Code?

1. **Ownership Transfer**: The variable `s1` owns the string
    `"Hello, Rust!"`. When `s1` is passed to the
    `take_ownership` function, ownership of the string is
    transferred to `s2`. After this, `s1` is no longer valid, and trying
    to use it would result in a compile-time error.

2. **Borrowing**: In the `print_string` function, we borrow the
    string `s2` as an immutable reference (`&s2`). This means that
    we can read from the string but not modify it. Rust allows
    multiple immutable references to exist at the same time
    without any issues.

3. **Mutable Borrowing**: The `change_string` function takes a
    mutable reference to the string `s3`. By passing `&mut s3`, we
    allow `change_string` to modify the original string. Since
    only one mutable reference to the data can exist at a time,
    Rust ensures that no other part of the program can modify or
    read from the string during this period.

The hands-on project illustrates how Rust's ownership model works in practice. The key takeaway here is that ownership and borrowing allow data to be shared safely without needing a garbage collector, and these principles are strictly enforced by the Rust compiler.

Wrapping Up

Rust's ownership model may seem strict at first, but it provides powerful guarantees about memory safety and concurrency. By enforcing rules around ownership, borrowing, and lifetimes at compile time, Rust ensures that your programs are free from common bugs like null pointer dereferencing, memory leaks, and dangling references. These safety checks are enforced without introducing runtime overhead, making Rust an ideal language for building performance-critical applications.

In the next chapters, we'll explore more advanced topics, such as working with Rust's concurrency model, error handling, and best practices for writing idiomatic Rust code. But for now, you should have a solid understanding of Rust's memory management system and how it ensures the safety and efficiency of your programs. The hands-on projects you've worked on here will lay the foundation for the more complex systems you'll build as you continue learning Rust.

Chapter 3: Data Types and Collections in Rust

Primitive Data Types: Integers, Floats, Booleans, Characters, and More

In any programming language, understanding the fundamental data types is essential because they form the building blocks for all the operations you perform in your code. In Rust, just like other languages, the core data types allow you to represent numbers, logical values, characters, and other basic structures in memory. Rust takes a strongly-typed approach to ensure safety and correctness, meaning every variable you declare must have a type, and that type cannot change once set.

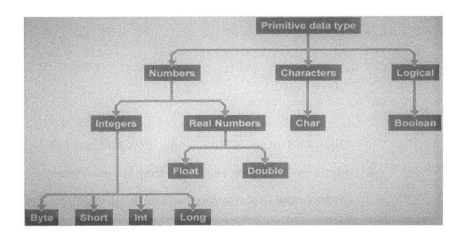

Rust has a variety of primitive data types, each of which is optimized for performance and memory usage. Here's a breakdown of the most commonly used primitive types in Rust.

1. **Integers (i32, u32, etc.):** Integers in Rust come in signed (`i`) and unsigned (`u`) varieties, and the size of the integer (in bits) is part of the type as well. The default integer type is `i32`, which is a signed 32-bit integer, meaning it can store both positive and negative whole numbers.

   - **Signed integers:** These allow both positive and negative values. The common signed integer types are `i8`, `i16`, `i32`, `i64`, and `i128`, where the number indicates how many bits are used to store the number. The signed integers have the prefix `i`, which stands for "integer" with the ability to store negative values.

   rust

   ```
   let x: i32 = -10;
   let y: i64 = 1000;
   ```

   - **Unsigned integers:** These only represent positive numbers (including zero), and they are used when you are sure that a number will never go negative. The unsigned integer types are `u8`, `u16`, `u32`, `u64`, and `u128`.

```rust
let a: u32 = 1000;
let b: u8 = 255; // Max value for u8
```

The size of the integer is important when optimizing for performance. For example, using `i8` instead of `i32` might save memory if your application deals with lots of small numbers.

2. **Floats (f32, f64)**: Rust has two primary floating-point types: `f32` (32-bit) and `f64` (64-bit). The default type for floating-point numbers is `f64`, which offers better precision at the cost of using more memory.

```rust
let pi: f64 = 3.14159;
let temp: f32 = 37.5;
```

When deciding between `f32` and `f64`, the main factor is the level of precision required. If you don't need high precision, and memory usage is a concern, use `f32`. For most scientific or financial calculations, `f64` is the better choice.

3. **Booleans (bool)**: Rust's boolean type, `bool`, represents either `true` or `false`. It is commonly used for control flow and condition checking.

rust

```
let is_active: bool = true;
let is_logged_in: bool = false;
```

4. **Characters (char)**: The `char` type in Rust is used to represent a single Unicode character. Unlike some languages, Rust's `char` type is not just a single byte but a 32-bit value that can represent any Unicode character.

rust

```
let letter: char = 'A';
let emoji: char = '😊';
```

This Unicode support makes Rust ideal for working with internationalized applications and ensures that it can represent a wide variety of characters.

5. **Tuples**: A tuple is a general-purpose container for storing multiple values of different types in a single compound type. Tuples are fixed-size and can store data of different types.

Rust allows you to access the elements of a tuple either by position or by destructuring.

rust

```
let tuple: (i32, f64, char) = (500, 3.14, 'a');
let (x, y, z) = tuple; // Destructuring
println!("x = {}, y = {}, z = {}", x, y, z);
```

Tuples are great for returning multiple values from a function or grouping related data together.

6. **Arrays**: Arrays in Rust are fixed-size collections of elements of the same type. They are a basic data structure but can be extremely useful when you know the exact number of elements you need to store. The type of the array includes the type of its elements and the number of elements it contains.

rust

```
let arr: [i32; 5] = [1, 2, 3, 4, 5];
let first = arr[0]; // Accessing an element
```

The fixed size makes arrays different from more flexible collections like vectors, but they are still useful for certain types of operations that require a known and constant number of elements.

Working with Strings and Arrays: String Slices, Mutable and Immutable Arrays

Strings in Rust are a little more complex than simple arrays, but they are essential for working with text. Rust provides two primary ways to work with strings: string literals and `String` objects.

1. **String Literals and String Types**:
   - **String Literals**: String literals are immutable slices of strings that are stored directly in the program's binary, making them fast but inflexible. They have a fixed length and cannot be changed once created.

     rust

     ```rust
     let hello = "Hello, world!"; // This is a
     string slice
     ```

   - **String Objects**: A `String` is a growable, heap-allocated string type that can be modified after creation. It is more flexible than string literals, and you can append, remove, and modify its contents.

     rust

     ```rust
     let mut s = String::from("Hello");
     s.push_str(", world!");
     ```

The key difference is that `String` can be mutated, whereas string literals are immutable.

2. **String Slices**: A **string slice** is a reference to a part of a string, and it is a view into a sequence of characters in a `String` or string literal. String slices are used when you need to reference a part of a string without taking ownership of it.

rust

```
let s = String::from("Hello, Rust!");
let slice = &s[0..5]; // Borrowing a slice from
the string
```

String slices are useful when you need to work with only part of a string but don't need the overhead of ing the data into a new `String`.

3. **Mutable and Immutable Arrays**: Arrays in Rust are fixed in size, and their elements must all be of the same type. You can have both immutable and mutable arrays, depending on whether or not you need to modify the array's contents after initialization.

   o **Immutable Array:**

```rust
rust
```

```rust
let arr: [i32; 3] = [1, 2, 3];
```

o **Mutable Array:**

```rust
rust
```

```rust
let mut arr: [i32; 3] = [1, 2, 3];
arr[0] = 10;
```

4. Rust guarantees safety with both immutable and mutable arrays, ensuring that no out-of-bounds access occurs at runtime. Accessing elements is done using indices.

Vectors and Hash Maps: Using Vectors and Hash Maps for Flexible Storage

1. **Vectors (Vec):** A vector is a growable array in Rust. Unlike arrays, vectors can change size dynamically as you add or remove elements. They are commonly used when you need a collection of items but don't know the exact number in advance.

    o Creating a new vector:

```rust
rust
```

```rust
let mut v: Vec<i32> = Vec::new();
v.push(1);
v.push(2);
v.push(3);
```

o Accessing elements:

```rust
rust
```

```rust
let first = v[0]; // Accessing the first
element
```

o Vectors are often used because they provide dynamic resizing and the ability to manage memory efficiently. Their size and contents are determined at runtime, and Rust ensures that vectors are always properly managed in terms of memory.

2. **Hash Maps (HashMap)**: Hash maps are a collection type that stores data in key-value pairs, allowing you to quickly access values based on a specific key. Rust's `HashMap` is part of the `std::collections` module.

   o Creating a new hash map:

```rust
rust
```

```rust
use std::collections::HashMap;
```

```rust
let mut map = HashMap::new();
map.insert("name", "Alice");
map.insert("age", "30");
```

- o   Accessing values in a hash map:

```
rust
```

```rust
let name = map.get("name");
match name {
    Some(v) => println!("Name: {}", v),
    None => println!("Key not found"),
}
```

3. Hash maps are powerful for storing data that can be accessed via unique keys. They are commonly used in applications where you need fast lookups or need to organize data based on some identifier.

Hands-on Project: Build a Program that Processes and Stores User Input in Vectors and Hash Maps

Let's put what we've learned into practice by building a program that processes user input and stores the data in vectors and hash maps.

For this project, we'll write a simple contact manager that allows the user to enter names and phone numbers, and stores them in a vector. The program will then allow the user to look up contacts by name using a hash map.

Here's the code for the contact manager:

```rust
use std::collections::HashMap;
use std::io;

fn main() {
    let mut contacts: HashMap<String, String> =
HashMap::new();
    let mut names: Vec<String> = Vec::new();

    loop {
        println!("Enter a command (add, list,
quit):");
        let mut command = String::new();
        io::stdin().read_line(&mut
command).expect("Failed to read line");
        let command = command.trim();

        match command {
            "add" => {
                println!("Enter name:");
```

```rust
            let mut name = String::new();
            io::stdin().read_line(&mut
name).expect("Failed to read line");
            let name = name.trim().to_string();

            println!("Enter phone number:");
            let mut phone = String::new();
            io::stdin().read_line(&mut
phone).expect("Failed to read line");
            let phone = phone.trim().to_string();

            contacts.insert(name.clone(), phone);
            names.push(name);
        }
        "list" => {
            println!("Contacts:");
            for name in &names {
                if let Some(phone) =
contacts.get(name) {
                    println!("{}: {}", name,
phone);
                }
            }
        }
        "quit" => break,
        _ => println!("Invalid command"),
    }
    }
}
```

What's Happening in the Code?

1. **Storing Contacts**: We use a `HashMap` to store the contacts, where the key is the contact's name (a `String`), and the value is the phone number (another `String`).

2. **Names Vector**: We also use a `Vec` to keep track of the names of all the contacts in the order they were added. This allows us to list the contacts later.

3. **User Input**: The program prompts the user to either add a new contact, list the contacts, or quit. Depending on the user's input, the program either inserts a new contact into the `HashMap` and `Vec` or lists all the contacts.

This hands-on project demonstrates how Rust's collections—vectors and hash maps—can be used to store and process data. It also highlights how Rust's type system and memory safety features make working with these collections both efficient and secure.

Chapter 4: Control Flow and Error Handling

If-Else, Loops, and Match Expressions: Conditional Execution and Pattern Matching

Control flow is a fundamental concept in programming that determines the order in which the statements of your program are executed. In Rust, like most languages, control flow is governed by conditional statements, loops, and pattern matching. These constructs allow you to direct your program to perform different actions based on conditions, repeat tasks, and deconstruct data in a way that makes it easy to work with complex structures.

1. If-Else Statements

The `if-else` statement in Rust is similar to those in other languages, and it allows you to execute a block of code based on a condition. The condition is a boolean expression, and if it's true, the associated block of code will be executed.

Here's the basic syntax of an `if-else` statement in Rust:

```rust
let x = 10;

if x > 5 {
    println!("x is greater than 5");
} else {
    println!("x is not greater than 5");
}
```

In this example, the program checks if the value of x is greater than 5. If it is, it prints "x is greater than 5"; otherwise, it prints "x is not greater than 5". The conditional statement can be as complex as needed, using logical operators like && (AND) and || (OR).

Rust also allows for a more concise form of conditional expressions. Rust doesn't require parentheses around the condition in `if` statements, unlike some other languages like C or JavaScript, but you do need curly braces (`{}`) to denote blocks.

2. Loops in Rust

Rust provides three types of loops: `loop`, `while`, and `for`.

- **Loop**: The `loop` keyword creates an infinite loop, which continues until explicitly broken using the `break` keyword. This is often useful for creating repeatable tasks or retry logic.

rust

```rust
let mut counter = 0;

loop {
    counter += 1;
    println!("Counter is: {}", counter);
    if counter == 5 {
        break;
    }
}
```

In this example, the program will loop indefinitely, incrementing the `counter` variable and printing its value, until `counter` reaches 5. At that point, the loop terminates with the `break` keyword.

- **While Loop:** The `while` loop runs as long as the condition evaluates to `true`. It's more like traditional loops you might see in other languages.

rust

```rust
let mut counter = 0;

while counter < 5 {
    println!("Counter is: {}", counter);
    counter += 1;
```

```
}
```

This loop continues as long as `counter` is less than 5. Once `counter` becomes 5 or greater, the loop exits.

- **For Loop**: The `for` loop in Rust is typically used to iterate over collections, like arrays or vectors. It provides a way to loop over elements directly without needing to manage an index.

rust

```
let numbers = vec![1, 2, 3, 4, 5];

for num in numbers {
    println!("{}", num);
}
```

This loop iterates over each element in the vector `numbers`, printing each number to the console.

You can also use ranges with `for` loops, which are handy for looping through a sequence of numbers:

rust

```
for i in 0..5 {
    println!("{}", i);
```

```
}
```

This will print the numbers 0 through 4 (inclusive of the starting point, exclusive of the ending point).

3. Match Expressions

Rust's match expression is a powerful and expressive control flow tool that allows you to compare a value against multiple patterns. It's Rust's answer to switch statements in other languages, but it is much more robust, as it supports complex patterns and conditions.

Here's an example of using match with an integer value:

rust

```
let number = 2;

match number {
    1 => println!("One"),
    2 => println!("Two"),
    3 => println!("Three"),
    _ => println!("Other number"),  // _ acts as a
wildcard that catches all other cases
}
```

In this example, the program matches the value of number to the corresponding pattern and prints the matching output. If the value doesn't match any of the specific patterns (1, 2, 3), the wildcard pattern _ catches it, and the program prints "Other number".

`match` is especially useful when dealing with enums or complex data structures. Let's consider an example using an enum, which is a powerful Rust feature:

rust

```
enum Direction {
    Up,
    Down,
    Left,
    Right,
}

let direction = Direction::Left;

match direction {
    Direction::Up => println!("Moving up"),
    Direction::Down => println!("Moving down"),
    Direction::Left => println!("Moving left"),
    Direction::Right => println!("Moving right"),
}
```

In this case, `match` is used to handle the different variants of the `Direction` enum. This is one of the areas where `match` truly shines, as it allows you to pattern match on enums and other complex types in a way that makes your code easier to understand and less error-prone.

Rust's Error Handling Model: The Result and Option Types

Rust's error handling system is one of the key features that sets it apart from many other programming languages. Unlike many other languages that use exceptions, Rust handles errors through two powerful types: `Result` and `Option`. These types make it clear when something might go wrong and force you to handle potential failures explicitly.

1. The `Option` Type

The `Option` type is used when there might be a value or there might not. It is defined as:

rust

```
enum Option<T> {
    Some(T),
    None,
}
```

The `Option` type is used to represent the concept of a value that may or may not exist. For example, when accessing a value in a map or performing a calculation that might fail, you often end up with an `Option`. The two variants are:

- **Some(T)**: Represents a value of type `T`.
- **None**: Represents the absence of a value.

Here's how you can use `Option` in practice:

rust

```
let some_number: Option<i32> = Some(10);
let no_number: Option<i32> = None;

match some_number {
    Some(value) => println!("The value is: {}",
value),
    None => println!("No value found"),
}
```

In this example, we use a `match` expression to handle both the `Some` and `None` variants. If the `Option` is `Some`, we print the value; if it's `None`, we print a different message.

The `Option` type is incredibly useful when working with functions that might fail or return nothing, such as looking up a key in a hash map or searching for an element in a collection.

2. The `Result` Type

The `Result` type is used for functions that can succeed or fail, where success returns a value and failure provides an error. It is defined as:

rust

```rust
enum Result<T, E> {
    Ok(T),
    Err(E),
}
```

- **Ok(T)**: Represents success and contains a value of type `T`.
- **Err(E)**: Represents failure and contains an error of type `E`.

The `Result` type is commonly used for functions that can fail due to external factors, such as file I/O, network communication, or user input. For example:

rust

```rust
use std::fs::File;
use std::io::{self, Read};

fn read_file(file_path: &str) -> Result<String,
io::Error> {
    let mut file = File::open(file_path)?; // Using
the `?` operator to propagate errors
    let mut contents = String::new();
```

```
    file.read_to_string(&mut contents)?;
    Ok(contents)
}
```

In this example, the `read_file` function returns a `Result` type. If the file is successfully opened and read, it returns an `Ok` containing the file's contents. If an error occurs (like the file not existing), it returns an `Err` with an error message.

You can use `match` or combinators like `.unwrap()`, `.map()`, or `.and_then()` to handle the result. However, Rust encourages explicit handling of `Result` values, making it clear when a function can potentially fail.

3. Unwrapping and Pattern Matching: Safe Handling of Errors and Options

Rust provides mechanisms to deal with `Option` and `Result` types in a safe way, such as using `unwrap`, `expect`, or better yet, handling the values properly with pattern matching or combinators.

- **Unwrapping**: The `unwrap()` method is used to get the value inside an `Option` or `Result`, but it will panic if the value is `None` or `Err`. It should be used carefully and only when you're sure the value will not be absent or erroneous.

```rust
let value = Some(10);
let x = value.unwrap();   // This works fine
```

But if the `Option` is `None`, it will panic:

```rust
let no_value: Option<i32> = None;
let x = no_value.unwrap(); // This will panic
```

- **Pattern Matching**: The safest and most idiomatic way to handle `Option` and `Result` is with pattern matching. This allows you to handle all possible cases in a structured and predictable way.

```rust
let some_number: Option<i32> = Some(10);

match some_number {
    Some(value) => println!("The value is: {}", value),
    None => println!("No value found"),
}
```

- **Expect:** The `expect()` method is similar to `unwrap()`, but it allows you to provide a custom error message if the value is absent. This is more informative than the default panic message from `unwrap()`.

```rust
```

```rust
let value = Some(10);
let x = value.expect("Expected a value, but found None");
```

Hands-on Project: Build a Simple Command-Line Tool That Uses Control Flow and Error Handling for User Input

Now that you have a solid understanding of control flow and error handling, let's build a simple command-line tool that prompts the user for input, processes that input, and handles potential errors gracefully. Our tool will ask the user to input their age, and we will validate that the input is a valid number.

```rust
```

```rust
use std::io::{self, Write};

fn main() {
    println!("Please enter your age:");

    let mut age_input = String::new();
```

```
    io::stdin().read_line(&mut
age_input).expect("Failed to read line");

    let age: Result<i32, _> =
age_input.trim().parse();

    match age {
        Ok(age) if age >= 18 => println!("You are an
adult, age: {}", age),
        Ok(age) => println!("You are a minor, age:
{}", age),
        Err(_) => println!("Invalid input, please
enter a valid number"),
    }
}
```

What's Happening in the Code?

1. **User Input**: The program first asks the user to enter their age and reads the input into a string variable. The `read_line()` function is used to capture input from the user. It returns a `Result`, which is why we use `expect()` to handle any possible errors (like input failure).

2. **Error Handling**: We attempt to parse the user's input into an integer using the `parse()` method, which returns a `Result`. The `Result` type allows us to handle cases where the input cannot be converted to an integer (e.g., if the user enters non-numeric data).

3. **Pattern Matching**: Using a `match` expression, we handle the
    valid input case by checking if the input represents an age of
    18 or older. We also handle errors gracefully by printing an
    error message if the input is invalid.

By using pattern matching with the `Result` type, we ensure that our
program can handle user input errors in a safe and predictable way.

This chapter covered essential control flow concepts in Rust,
including `if-else`, loops, and `match` expressions. We also explored
Rust's error handling model with the `Result` and `Option` types,
which provide a safe and explicit way to handle potential errors. With
the hands-on project, you've seen how to build a simple command-
line tool that handles errors and user input using control flow,
ensuring that your code is both reliable and safe. As you continue
your journey with Rust, these fundamental techniques will form the
basis for writing more complex and robust applications.

Chapter 5: Structs, Enums, and Pattern Matching

Defining Structs: Creating Custom Data Types

Rust is a systems programming language that emphasizes safety and performance. One of its most powerful features is the ability to define custom data types using **structs**. Structs allow you to group related data together under one name, making it easier to manage and manipulate complex data in a way that is both efficient and type-safe. Structs are crucial in building real-world systems, as they allow you to define and work with more meaningful, descriptive types.

A **struct** in Rust is a way to define a custom data type that can hold multiple values of different types. Structs are used to create complex data structures, such as a `Point` in a 2D space or a `Book` with attributes like title and author.

1. Defining a Simple Struct

Rust provides a straightforward way to define a struct. The basic syntax is as follows:

```rust
struct Point {
    x: i32,
    y: i32,
}
```

In this example, we've defined a struct named `Point`, which has two fields: `x` and `y`, both of which are of type `i32`. The fields of a struct are accessed using dot notation:

```rust
let p = Point { x: 10, y: 20 };
println!("The point is at ({}, {})", p.x, p.y);
```

Here, `p` is an instance of the `Point` struct, and we can access the `x` and `y` fields of the point using `p.x` and `p.y`. This allows us to group related data (the `x` and `y` coordinates) into a single unit.

2. Structs with Methods

In addition to holding data, structs in Rust can also have associated functions, often called methods. These methods can be used to modify or interact with the data stored within the struct. Rust does not support traditional object-oriented classes, but methods on structs allow us to encapsulate behavior within a type.

To define methods on a struct, you define an `impl` block for the struct. Here's an example:

```rust
struct Point {
    x: i32,
    y: i32,
}

impl Point {
    // Method to calculate the distance from another point
    fn distance_from_origin(&self) -> f64 {
        ((self.x.pow(2) + self.y.pow(2)) as f64).sqrt()
    }
}

let p = Point { x: 3, y: 4 };
println!("The distance from the origin is {}", p.distance_from_origin());
```

In this case, the method `distance_from_origin` calculates the Euclidean distance from the origin (0, 0) to the point. The `&self` syntax indicates that the method borrows the struct, meaning it does not take ownership of the struct.

3. Tuple Structs

Rust also supports **tuple structs**, which are a variant of regular structs that do not require field names. Instead, the fields are accessed by their position within the struct, similar to a tuple. Tuple structs are useful when you have a simple, untagged grouping of values.

Here's an example of a tuple struct:

```rust
struct Color(u8, u8, u8); // Representing RGB color

let black = Color(0, 0, 0);
println!("Black color: ({}, {}, {})", black.0,
black.1, black.2);
```

In this case, the `Color` struct holds three `u8` values representing the red, green, and blue components of a color. The fields are accessed using positional indexing (`black.0`, `black.1`, `black.2`).

Enums in Rust: Working with Enums to Model Different Possibilities

While structs are great for grouping related data, **enums** allow us to define types that can take one of several possible values. An enum is a type that can have multiple, defined variants, and each variant can optionally hold data of different types.

Rust enums are very powerful and provide a way to model complex possibilities in a way that is both expressive and type-safe.

1. Defining Enums

An enum in Rust is defined using the `enum` keyword. You can define multiple variants, and each variant can hold associated data. Here's a basic example:

rust

```
enum Direction {
    Up,
    Down,
    Left,
    Right,
}
```

In this example, the `Direction` enum has four variants: `Up`, `Down`, `Left`, and `Right`. Each variant is a simple unit-like enum, meaning it doesn't hold any associated data.

To use the enum, you can instantiate it like this:

rust

```
let direction = Direction::Up;
match direction {
    Direction::Up => println!("Going up!"),
    Direction::Down => println!("Going down!"),
    Direction::Left => println!("Going left!"),
    Direction::Right => println!("Going right!"),
}
```

2. Enums with Data

Rust enums can also hold data, making them even more powerful.
For example, each direction in the Direction enum could also hold
a distance value:

rust

```
enum Direction {
    Up(i32),
    Down(i32),
    Left(i32),
    Right(i32),
}
```

Now, each variant of Direction holds an i32 value representing a
distance. You can use pattern matching to extract the data from
each variant:

rust

```
let move_up = Direction::Up(10);
match move_up {
    Direction::Up(distance) => println!("Moving up by
{} units", distance),
    Direction::Down(distance) => println!("Moving
down by {} units", distance),
    Direction::Left(distance) => println!("Moving
left by {} units", distance),
    Direction::Right(distance) => println!("Moving
right by {} units", distance),
}
```

In this case, the `Up`, `Down`, `Left`, and `Right` variants now carry the distance value, allowing us to pass more information through the enum.

3. Enums with Multiple Types of Data

Rust enums can hold different types of data for each variant. For example, the `Direction` enum might hold different types of data depending on the variant, such as a string or a tuple:

rust

```
enum Direction {
    Up(i32),
    Down(i32),
```

```
    Left(String),
    Right { x: i32, y: i32 },
}
```

In this example:

- Up and Down hold an i32 (distance),
- Left holds a String (name of the place),
- Right holds a struct-like value with x and y coordinates.

Each variant of the enum can contain data of different types, and you can pattern match accordingly:

rust

```
let move_left = Direction::Left(String::from("Left
Corner"));
let move_right = Direction::Right { x: 10, y: 20 };

match move_left {
    Direction::Up(distance) => println!("Moving up by
{} units", distance),
    Direction::Down(distance) => println!("Moving
down by {} units", distance),
    Direction::Left(place) => println!("Moving to the
left: {}", place),
    Direction::Right { x, y } => println!("Moving
right to coordinates ({}, {})", x, y),
}
```

Pattern Matching: Using `match` to Destructure Enums and Other Complex Types

Pattern matching is one of the most powerful features of Rust. It allows you to compare a value against patterns and execute code based on which pattern the value matches. Rust's `match` expression is highly expressive and supports complex patterns, making it ideal for handling enums.

1. Basic Pattern Matching

When you use `match`, you typically compare a value against multiple patterns, each of which can have an associated block of code. Here's a simple `match` with an enum:

rust

```rust
enum Status {
    Active,
    Inactive,
    Suspended,
}

let user_status = Status::Active;

match user_status {
    Status::Active => println!("The user is active"),
```

```
    Status::Inactive => println!("The user is
inactive"),
    Status::Suspended => println!("The user is
suspended"),
}
```

In this example, `match` compares `user_status` to each variant of the `Status` enum and executes the corresponding block.

2. Matching with Structs and Enums

Pattern matching is especially useful with enums that contain data. When you define an enum variant with data, you can destructure that data in the `match` arms:

rust

```
enum Direction {
    Up(i32),
    Down(i32),
    Left(String),
    Right { x: i32, y: i32 },
}

let direction = Direction::Right { x: 10, y: 20 };

match direction {
    Direction::Up(distance) => println!("Moving up by
{} units", distance),
```

```
    Direction::Down(distance) => println!("Moving
down by {} units", distance),
    Direction::Left(place) => println!("Moving to the
left: {}", place),
    Direction::Right { x, y } => println!("Moving
right to coordinates ({}, {})", x, y),
}
```

In this example, the `Right` variant holds a struct-like value with `x` and `y`. When matching this variant, we can destructure it directly in the `match` expression to access the `x` and `y` values.

Hands-on Project: A Basic App that Models a Library System Using Structs and Enums

Let's apply what we've learned by building a simple library system using structs and enums. This system will allow you to store books, borrow books, and check their availability.

1. **Structs**: We'll define a `Book` struct to store book information and a `Library` struct to manage the collection of books.
2. **Enums**: We'll use an enum to represent the status of a book (whether it is available or borrowed).
3. **Pattern Matching**: We'll use pattern matching to handle the borrowing process.

Here's the code for our library system:

```rust

#[derive(Debug)]
enum BookStatus {
    Available,
    Borrowed(String), // Holds the name of the
borrower
}

#[derive(Debug)]
struct Book {
    title: String,
    author: String,
    status: BookStatus,
}

struct Library {
    books: Vec<Book>,
}

impl Library {
    fn new() -> Library {
        Library { books: Vec::new() }
    }

    fn add_book(&mut self, title: String, author:
String) {
        let book = Book {
            title,
```

```
                author,
                status: BookStatus::Available,
            };
            self.books.push(book);
        }


    fn borrow_book(&mut self, title: &str, borrower:
String) {
        for book in &mut self.books {
            if book.title == title {
                match book.status {
                    BookStatus::Available => {
                        book.status =
BookStatus::Borrowed(borrower);
                        println!("You have borrowed:
{}", title);
                    }
                    BookStatus::Borrowed(ref
borrower_name) => {
                        println!("Sorry, {} is
already borrowed by {}", title, borrower_name);
                    }
                }
            }
        }
    }


    fn return_book(&mut self, title: &str) {
        for book in &mut self.books {
```

```
            if book.title == title {
                match book.status {
                    BookStatus::Borrowed(_) => {
                        book.status =
BookStatus::Available;
                        println!("You have returned:
{}", title);
                    }
                    BookStatus::Available => {
                        println!("This book is not
borrowed yet.");
                    }
                }
            }
        }
    }
}

fn main() {
    let mut library = Library::new();
    library.add_book(String::from("The Catcher in the
Rye"), String::from("J.D. Salinger"));
    library.add_book(String::from("1984"),
String::from("George Orwell"));

    library.borrow_book("1984",
String::from("Alice"));
    library.return_book("1984");
    library.borrow_book("1984", String::from("Bob"));
```

}

What's Happening in the Code?

1. **Structs**: We define a `Book` struct to represent the properties of a book. It holds the title, author, and a `BookStatus`, which tells us whether the book is available or borrowed.

2. **Enums**: The `BookStatus` enum helps us track whether a book is available or borrowed. If a book is borrowed, the `Borrowed` variant holds the name of the borrower.

3. **Library Management**: The `Library` struct holds a vector of books. It provides methods to add books, borrow them, and return them. We use pattern matching to handle the different statuses of a book when borrowing or returning it.

By building this project, you've seen how structs and enums come together to model a real-world system and how pattern matching allows for more expressive, readable code when dealing with different states or conditions.

Chapter 6: Functions and Closures

Functions and closures are two essential building blocks of Rust. They allow you to organize your code into reusable and flexible components, enabling you to break down complex tasks into manageable parts. While functions are a staple of programming, closures provide a more flexible way of handling behavior dynamically at runtime. This chapter will dive deep into defining functions, understanding closures, and exploring higher-order functions. Along the way, we will walk through hands-on examples and projects to illustrate these concepts in real-world applications.

Defining Functions: Understanding Function Signatures, Return Types, and Parameters

Functions are fundamental to any programming language, and Rust is no exception. A function allows you to encapsulate a block of code that can be reused multiple times, improving code readability and modularity. In Rust, defining a function involves specifying the function's name, its parameters (if any), and its return type (if any).

1. Basic Syntax of Functions

The basic syntax for defining a function in Rust is as follows:

```rust
fn function_name(parameter1: Type1, parameter2:
Type2) -> ReturnType {
    // function body
}
```

Let's break down the components:

- `fn` is the keyword used to declare a function.
- `function_name` is the name of the function.
- `(parameter1: Type1, parameter2: Type2)` is a list of parameters. Each parameter has a name and a type.
- `-> ReturnType` specifies the type of the value the function will return. If the function does not return anything, this is omitted or replaced with `->` `()` (unit type).

2. Function Parameters and Return Types

Parameters are the inputs to a function, and they can be of any type that is valid in Rust. Parameters are always explicitly typed, meaning that you must specify the type for each parameter when defining the function.

rust

```rust
fn add_numbers(a: i32, b: i32) -> i32 {
    a + b
}
```

In this example:

- a and b are the parameters, and both are of type i32.
- The function returns an i32 value, which is the sum of a and b.

In Rust, if the function doesn't return any value, you don't need to include a return type:

rust

```rust
fn print_message(message: &str) {
    println!("{}", message);
}
```

Here, the function print_message takes a single &str parameter (a string slice) and doesn't return anything. The function's return type is implicitly (), which represents an empty unit type indicating no value.

3. Returning Values from Functions

Rust functions are designed to return values explicitly, and there are a few ways to do this:

1. **Returning a value explicitly with the `return` keyword**: The `return` keyword is used to return a value from a function. This can be helpful when you want to break out of the function early.

    rust

    ```rust
    fn multiply(x: i32, y: i32) -> i32 {
        return x * y; // explicitly returns the
    product of x and y
    }
    ```

2. **Implicit return**: In Rust, you can also return a value implicitly by omitting the `return` keyword. In this case, the last expression in the function is automatically returned.

    rust

    ```rust
    fn multiply(x: i32, y: i32) -> i32 {
        x * y // implicitly returns the product of
    x and y
    }
    ```

1. The `Unit` Type (`()`)

In Rust, the unit type `()` represents an empty value or the absence of a return value. It is the default return type for functions that don't explicitly return a value. The function's body may contain code that performs side effects (such as printing to the console), but it doesn't provide any result that other parts of the program can use.

rust

```rust
fn say_hello() -> () {
    println!("Hello, world!");
}
```

In the example above, the function `say_hello` doesn't return anything meaningful, so it's implied that it returns the unit type `()`.

Closures: Anonymous Functions and Their Use Cases

Closures are one of the most powerful features in Rust. A **closure** is a function that can capture its surrounding environment and be passed around as a first-class citizen. Closures are anonymous, meaning they don't require a name, and they can be defined inline.

1. Basic Syntax of Closures

Closures in Rust have a syntax similar to that of functions, but with a few key differences:

rust

```
let closure_name = |parameter1, parameter2| ->
ReturnType {
    // closure body
};
```

Here's an example of a closure that takes two i32 values and returns their sum:

rust

```
let add = |x: i32, y: i32| -> i32 {
    x + y
};

let result = add(2, 3);
println!("The sum is: {}", result);
```

In this case:

- |x: i32, y: i32| is the list of parameters.
- The closure body is the expression x + y.
- add is a closure that can be called like a function.

2. Capturing Variables

One of the unique features of closures is their ability to capture variables from their surrounding environment. Rust has three types of closures based on how they capture variables: by reference, by mutable reference, or by value.

1. **By Reference**: When a closure captures a variable by reference, it borrows the variable immutably.

   rust

   ```
   let x = 10;
   let closure = || println!("x is: {}", x);
   closure();
   ```

2. **By Mutable Reference**: Closures can also capture variables by mutable reference, allowing them to modify the captured variable.

   rust

   ```
   let mut x = 10;
   let mut closure = || {
       x += 5;
       println!("x is now: {}", x);
   };
   closure();
   ```

3. **By Value**: The closure can take ownership of a variable and move it inside the closure.

```rust
let s = String::from("Hello");
let closure = move || {
    println!("{}", s);
};
closure();
```

In this case, `move` forces the closure to take ownership of `s`, meaning `s` is no longer available outside the closure.

3. Use Cases for Closures

Closures are incredibly useful in Rust for a variety of scenarios:

- **Callbacks**: You can use closures as callbacks that execute custom behavior.
- **Functional Programming**: Closures allow you to pass functions as arguments to other functions, enabling higher-order programming.
- **Iterators**: Rust's iterator combinators use closures to transform and filter data.

Higher-Order Functions: Passing Functions as Arguments and Returning Functions

Higher-order functions are functions that take other functions as arguments or return functions. Rust's support for closures makes it easy to define higher-order functions that operate on other functions.

1. Passing Functions as Arguments

A higher-order function can take a closure (or function) as an argument. Here's an example of a higher-order function that accepts a closure that processes a number:

rust

```
fn apply<F>(f: F)
where
    F: Fn(i32) -> i32
{
    let result = f(5);
    println!("Result: {}", result);
}

let square = |x| x * x;
apply(square);
```

In this example:

- `apply` takes a closure `f` that accepts an `i32` and returns an `i32`.
- `square` is passed as an argument to `apply`, and `apply` executes `square(5)`.

2. Returning Functions from Functions

Rust also supports returning functions from other functions. This is commonly used when creating specialized closures based on parameters. Here's an example:

rust

```rust
fn multiplier(factor: i32) -> impl Fn(i32) -> i32 {
    move |x| x * factor
}

let multiply_by_2 = multiplier(2);
let result = multiply_by_2(10);
println!("10 multiplied by 2 is {}", result);
```

In this example, `multiplier` is a higher-order function that returns a closure. The returned closure takes an `i32` and multiplies it by the `factor` passed to `multiplier`.

Hands-on Project: Build a Utility that Processes a List of Items Using Closures

Let's put everything we've learned into practice by building a utility that processes a list of items using closures. Our utility will take a list of integers and apply various transformations (such as doubling the values, squaring them, etc.) using closures.

rust

```rust
fn process_list<F>(list: Vec<i32>, operation: F) ->
Vec<i32>
where
    F: Fn(i32) -> i32,
{
    list.into_iter().map(operation).collect()
}

fn main() {
    let numbers = vec![1, 2, 3, 4, 5];

    let doubled = process_list(numbers.clone(), |x| x
* 2);
    println!("Doubled: {:?}", doubled);

    let squared = process_list(numbers, |x| x * x);
    println!("Squared: {:?}", squared);
}
```

What's Happening in the Code?

1. **Higher-Order Function `process_list`:**
   - `process_list` takes a vector of integers (`Vec<i32>`) and a closure (`operation`).
   - It applies the closure to each element in the list using `.map()` and returns a new list with the transformed values.
   - The closure is passed as an argument, allowing you to dynamically decide what operation to perform on the list.

2. **Transformation with Closures:**
   - We apply two different closures to the same list: one that doubles each element (`|x| x * 2`), and one that squares each element (`|x| x * x`).
   - This demonstrates how closures can be used to create reusable, customizable transformations that are passed as arguments.

3. **Functional Approach:**
   - The use of `map()` and closures gives the code a functional programming flavor, where you describe the transformation of data declaratively instead of imperatively.

Conclusion

In this chapter, we've explored how Rust's functions and closures give you powerful tools to write modular, reusable, and flexible code. We've learned how to define functions, pass them around as arguments, return them from other functions, and work with closures to capture and manipulate variables from the surrounding scope. Closures provide a way to write highly customizable code, making them invaluable for tasks that require dynamic behavior.

By working through the hands-on project, you've gained practical experience with closures and higher-order functions. These concepts are integral to mastering Rust and will allow you to build sophisticated, efficient, and elegant solutions to problems. As you continue to explore Rust, you'll discover more ways to apply functions and closures to solve complex challenges in a clear and expressive manner.

Chapter 7: Concurrency in Rust

Why Concurrency in Rust is Safe: The Concurrency Model in Rust

Concurrency is a powerful technique that allows you to execute multiple tasks at the same time, making your programs more efficient, especially when dealing with I/O-bound or CPU-bound workloads. In many programming languages, working with concurrency can be challenging due to potential issues like data races, deadlocks, and inconsistent states. However, Rust approaches concurrency with a strong focus on safety, ensuring that multithreaded code can be written without common pitfalls, like memory corruption or unintended shared access.

Rust's concurrency model is based on the same principles that govern its memory safety, particularly the ownership and borrowing rules. These rules ensure that data is either owned by a single thread or safely shared between threads. The Rust compiler enforces these rules at compile time, meaning that you will never encounter certain classes of concurrency bugs, such as race conditions or memory leaks, once your code has compiled.

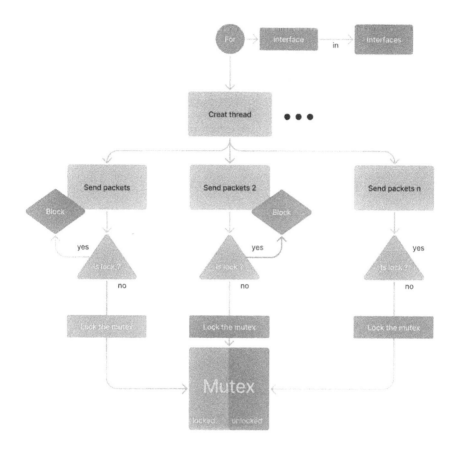

Rust achieves this safety through the following key principles:

- **Ownership and Borrowing**: The ownership system, which enforces that data can either be owned by one thread or borrowed immutably, is applied to concurrency as well. Rust ensures that mutable data is never shared between threads unless it is explicitly managed.

- **Thread Safety**: Rust ensures that data shared between threads is either immutable or mutable with controlled access, such as through locks or atomic operations.
- **Data Race Prevention**: Rust guarantees that mutable data cannot be shared between threads, preventing data races. At the same time, immutable data can be freely shared without risk of modification by another thread.

In short, Rust provides a robust foundation for writing concurrent programs, thanks to its design principles. You can work with threads, mutexes, and other concurrency tools, knowing that the compiler will catch errors before they ever run, reducing the chances of bugs that could potentially crash your program or cause unpredictable behavior.

Threads and Mutexes: How Rust Handles Multithreading

Rust provides built-in support for multithreading, enabling you to take full advantage of modern hardware with minimal overhead. Multithreading in Rust is built on the `std::thread` module, which allows you to create threads and manage their execution. However, multithreading is not the same as concurrent programming, as the latter focuses on the ability to make progress on multiple tasks at once, whereas multithreading focuses on executing multiple tasks at the same time.

1. Creating Threads in Rust

Creating a new thread in Rust is simple, thanks to the `thread::spawn` function. This function takes a closure as an argument, and the closure defines the code that will run in the new thread. Here's an example of spawning a thread to print a message:

rust

```
use std::thread;

fn main() {
    let handle = thread::spawn(|| {
        println!("Hello from a new thread!");
    });

    // Wait for the thread to finish execution
    handle.join().unwrap();
}
```

In this example:

- `thread::spawn` creates a new thread and executes the closure inside the thread.

- `handle.join()` is used to ensure that the main thread waits for the spawned thread to finish its execution before continuing. The `join` method blocks the calling thread until the thread represented by the `handle` finishes.

2. Accessing Shared Data Between Threads

Rust's ownership model ensures that data can either be owned by a single thread or shared immutably across threads. However, if you need to share mutable data across threads, you must explicitly manage access to this data using synchronization mechanisms like mutexes.

A **mutex** (short for "mutual exclusion") is a type of lock that ensures only one thread can access the data at a time. Rust provides the `std::sync::Mutex` type to handle this. A mutex ensures that if one thread is accessing the data, no other thread can access it until the lock is released.

Here's how to use a mutex in Rust:

rust

```
use std::sync::{Arc, Mutex};
use std::thread;

fn main() {
```

```
    let counter = Arc::new(Mutex::new(0)); // Arc
ensures the data can be shared across threads

    let mut handles = vec![];

    for _ in 0..10 {
        let counter = Arc::clone(&counter); // Clone
the Arc to get a reference to the data
        let handle = thread::spawn(move || {
            let mut num = counter.lock().unwrap(); //
Lock the mutex
            *num += 1;
        });
        handles.push(handle);
    }

    for handle in handles {
        handle.join().unwrap(); // Wait for all
threads to finish
    }

    println!("Result: {}", *counter.lock().unwrap());
// Print the final result
}
```

In this example:

- **Arc<Mutex<T>>**: The Arc (Atomic Reference Counting) type is used to enable multiple threads to share ownership of the data. `Arc` allows multiple threads to have references to the same data, but it's safe for concurrent access. The `Mutex` is used to ensure that only one thread can mutate the data at any given time.

- `counter.lock().unwrap()`: This method locks the mutex, ensuring that only one thread can access the data at a time. If a thread cannot obtain the lock, it will block until it becomes available.

- `handle.join().unwrap()`: This ensures that the main thread waits for all spawned threads to complete before printing the result.

This example demonstrates how Rust's concurrency model, combined with synchronization tools like `Mutex` and `Arc`, allows threads to safely share and modify data.

Channels: Using Rust's Channels for Communication Between Threads

In Rust, channels are a powerful way for threads to communicate with each other. A channel is a two-way communication system that allows you to send data from one thread to another. Rust provides a built-in `std::sync::mpsc` (multiple producer, single consumer) module for handling channels. The `mpsc` module is designed to send messages from multiple producers (threads) to a single consumer.

1. Creating and Using Channels

A channel consists of a sender and a receiver. The sender is used by the producing threads to send messages, and the receiver is used by the consuming thread to receive messages.

Here's an example of how to use channels in Rust:

rust

```
use std::sync::mpsc;
use std::thread;

fn main() {
    let (tx, rx) = mpsc::channel(); // Create a
channel
    let producer = thread::spawn(move || {
        tx.send("Hello from the producer").unwrap();
// Send a message through the channel
    });

    // Receive the message in the main thread
    let received = rx.recv().unwrap();
    println!("Received: {}", received);

    producer.join().unwrap(); // Wait for the
producer thread to finish
}
```

In this example:

- **mpsc::channel()**: This creates a new channel, returning a tuple containing a sender (tx) and a receiver (rx).
- **tx.send()**: The sender (tx) is used to send data over the channel.
- **rx.recv()**: The receiver (rx) is used to receive data from the channel. This blocks the main thread until a message is received.

2. Using Channels with Multiple Threads

You can also create multiple threads that each send data through the same channel. Here's an example with multiple producers sending messages to the same receiver:

rust

```
use std::sync::mpsc;
use std::thread;

fn main() {
    let (tx, rx) = mpsc::channel();
    let mut handles = vec![];

    for i in 0..5 {
        let tx = tx.clone(); // Clone the sender for
each thread
```

```
        let handle = thread::spawn(move || {
            let message = format!("Message from
thread {}", i);
            tx.send(message).unwrap(); // Send a
message from each thread
        });
        handles.push(handle);
    }

    for handle in handles {
        handle.join().unwrap();
    }

    // Receive and print all the messages
    for _ in 0..5 {
        let received = rx.recv().unwrap();
        println!("{}", received);
    }
}
```

In this case:

- We clone the sender (tx) for each thread, allowing them to send messages to the same receiver.
- The main thread receives messages from each of the threads, printing them out as they arrive.

Channels in Rust are a great way to synchronize and pass data between threads, ensuring safe communication with minimal overhead.

Hands-on Project: Building a Multithreaded Application that Fetches and Processes Data Concurrently

Let's build a simple multithreaded application that fetches and processes data concurrently. This app will simulate downloading data from multiple sources (represented by different URLs), and each thread will process the data as it arrives. For simplicity, the data fetching will be simulated with sleep calls.

The project will consist of:

1. **Fetching data concurrently using threads.**
2. **Using channels to pass the fetched data back to the main thread.**
3. **Processing the data in the main thread.**

Here's the code for the project:

```rust
use std::{thread, time};
```

```rust
use std::sync::mpsc;

fn fetch_data(url: &str) -> String {
    // Simulate a delay for fetching data
    thread::sleep(time::Duration::from_secs(2));
    format!("Data from {}", url)
}


fn main() {
    let (tx, rx) = mpsc::channel();
    let urls = vec![
        "http://example1.com",
        "http://example2.com",
        "http://example3.com",
    ];

    let mut handles = vec![];

    for url in urls {
        let tx = tx.clone();
        let handle = thread::spawn(move || {
            let data = fetch_data(url);
            tx.send(data).unwrap();
        });
        handles.push(handle);
    }

    for handle in handles {
        handle.join().unwrap();
```

```
    }

    // Process the fetched data
    for _ in 0..urls.len() {
        let data = rx.recv().unwrap();
        println!("Processed: {}", data);
    }
}
```

What's Happening in the Code?

1. **Fetching Data Concurrently**: We create multiple threads, each of which simulates fetching data from a different URL. The `fetch_data` function simulates a delay (using `thread::sleep`) to mimic real-world data fetching.

2. **Using Channels**: Each thread sends the fetched data through the channel to the main thread. The channel ensures that the main thread receives data safely and in order, even though the threads run concurrently.

3. **Processing Data**: Once the data is received in the main thread, it is printed as "processed." This represents the processing stage after the data is fetched and ready to be used.

Conclusion

Rust's concurrency model allows you to safely and efficiently manage multithreading in your applications. By leveraging Rust's ownership and borrowing rules, you can write concurrent programs that are free from data races and other common concurrency bugs. Rust provides robust tools for working with threads, mutexes, and channels, enabling safe and flexible concurrent programming.

In this chapter, you've learned how to:

- Create threads and spawn them for concurrent execution.
- Use mutexes to share mutable data safely across threads.
- Communicate between threads using channels.
- Build a practical multithreaded application that fetches and processes data concurrently.

These concurrency tools will help you write scalable, efficient, and safe multithreaded applications in Rust, whether you're handling I/O-bound tasks, CPU-intensive calculations, or more complex workflows. As you continue working with Rust, these concepts will become essential in building high-performance systems.

Chapter 8: Rust's Memory Management in Detail

Heap vs. Stack Memory: A Deep Dive into Memory Allocation

Memory management is one of the most critical components of any systems programming language. In most languages, memory management is abstracted away, but in Rust, developers have direct control over memory allocation, thanks to its unique ownership model. In this chapter, we'll dive into Rust's memory management, starting with the concepts of **heap** and **stack** memory. Understanding the differences between these two forms of memory allocation will give you a deeper appreciation of how Rust ensures safety and efficiency in its handling of memory.

1. The Stack

The **stack** is a region of memory where function call frames and local variables are stored. Each time a function is called, a new stack frame is created, and when the function exits, the stack frame is discarded. Stack memory is managed automatically, which means that when you declare a variable in a function, it is placed on the stack. The stack operates in a **LIFO** (Last In, First Out) manner, meaning the most recently added data is always the first to be removed.

In Rust, stack allocation is fast because memory is managed automatically and doesn't require complex algorithms to allocate or free memory. The stack stores data in contiguous blocks, and since stack frames are short-lived (they only exist for the duration of a function call), memory management is simple and efficient.

A key feature of stack memory is that it only holds data whose size is known at compile time. Variables like integers and floats, whose sizes are known ahead of time, are typically stored on the stack.

Example:

rust

```rust
fn example() {
    let x = 5;   // x is stored on the stack
    let y = 10; // y is also stored on the stack
    println!("x: {}, y: {}", x, y);
}
```

Here, both x and y are stored in the stack because their types and sizes are known at compile time.

2. The Heap

The **heap** is a region of memory that allows for dynamic memory allocation. When data needs to be allocated during runtime, rather than at compile time, it is placed on the heap. This allows programs to allocate memory dynamically based on the input size or requirements during execution.

Heap allocation is more expensive than stack allocation because it involves requesting memory from the operating system and later freeing it. When you allocate memory on the heap, you get a **pointer** to the allocated memory, but the actual data resides in a different location in memory. This introduces the need for more complex management, such as garbage collection (in other languages) or explicit memory management, as seen in Rust.

Rust does not have a garbage collector, but it uses its **ownership** system to ensure that memory on the heap is automatically freed when no longer needed.

Example:

rust

```
fn example() {
    let s = String::from("Hello, world!"); // `s` is
stored on the heap
```

```
println!("{}", s);
}
```

In this example, the `String` is allocated on the heap because it can grow or shrink in size dynamically, unlike a fixed-size array. The variable `s` is a pointer to the data on the heap.

3. Stack vs. Heap Summary

- **Stack:**
    - Fast allocation and deallocation.
    - Stores small, fixed-size data.
    - Memory is automatically freed when a function returns.
    - Used for data with a known, fixed size at compile time.
- **Heap:**
    - Slower allocation and deallocation.
    - Stores large, dynamically-sized data.
    - Memory must be explicitly managed, typically through ownership.
    - Used for data whose size is not known at compile time.

Rust's memory model uses both the stack and heap for different purposes. By default, Rust places simple data types on the stack and uses the heap for more complex, dynamically-sized data. Rust ensures that data is either owned by a single variable (stack-based) or managed via explicit ownership (heap-based), preventing common memory management errors like dangling pointers or double frees.

The Borrow Checker: Understanding How Rust Guarantees Memory Safety at Compile-Time

Rust's most powerful feature is its **ownership system**, which is enforced at compile time by the **borrow checker**. This system ensures that references to data are either mutable or immutable but never both simultaneously, preventing race conditions and memory safety issues that often occur in multi-threaded applications.

1. Ownership and Borrowing

In Rust, ownership is a strict rule: each piece of data has exactly one owner at any time. When the owner of the data goes out of scope, the memory is automatically freed. However, there are scenarios where multiple parts of your program need to access the same data. Rust uses **borrowing** to allow multiple references to data without violating memory safety.

There are two types of borrowing in Rust:

1. **Immutable Borrowing**: Allows multiple parts of your program to read data at the same time but prevents any modifications. Rust allows multiple immutable references (`&T`) to a piece of data at once because it is guaranteed that none of the references will modify the data.

   Example:

   rust

   ```
   let s = String::from("hello");
   let r1 = &s; // immutable borrow
   let r2 = &s; // immutable borrow
   println!("r1: {}, r2: {}", r1, r2); // both r1
   and r2 can be used to read `s`
   ```

2. **Mutable Borrowing**: Allows a single part of your program to modify data, but no other part can access the data during this time. This prevents data races because only one reference can have the ability to mutate the data.

   Example:

   rust

   ```
   let mut s = String::from("hello");
   let r1 = &mut s; // mutable borrow
   r1.push_str(", world");
   ```

```
println!("r1: {}", r1); // r1 can mutate `s`
```

Rust ensures that only one mutable reference exists at any time, preventing multiple parts of the program from mutating the same data simultaneously, thus preventing race conditions.

2. The Borrow Checker's Role

The borrow checker enforces Rust's ownership and borrowing rules. At compile time, it checks that:

- Data can only have one mutable reference or any number of immutable references at a time.
- Data is never accessed after it's been freed (i.e., no dangling references).
- There is no concurrent modification of data.

If you try to violate these rules, the Rust compiler will produce an error, preventing unsafe code from being executed.

Example of a borrow checker error:

rust

```
fn main() {
    let mut x = String::from("hello");
    let r1 = &x;
```

```
    let r2 = &mut x; // error: cannot borrow `x` as
mutable because it is also borrowed as immutable
}
```

In this case, the compiler catches the violation because you are trying to borrow x mutably while it is already borrowed immutably.

Lifetime Annotations: Using Lifetime Annotations to Manage References in Complex Programs

Lifetime annotations are a powerful feature in Rust that help the borrow checker track how long references to data are valid. Lifetimes prevent dangling references and ensure that data doesn't get destroyed while it's still being used by another part of the program.

1. Why Lifetimes Are Necessary

In Rust, references must always be valid. The borrow checker tracks references to ensure they do not outlive the data they point to. When dealing with complex data structures or functions with multiple references, it's often unclear to the compiler how long a reference should be valid. This is where lifetime annotations come in.

Consider the following example:

rust

```rust
fn longest<'a>(s1: &'a str, s2: &'a str) -> &'a str {
    if s1.len() > s2.len() {
        s1
    } else {
        s2
    }
}
```

Here:

- 'a is a **lifetime annotation**. It tells the compiler that both s1 and s2 must live at least as long as 'a (the lifetime of the function's return value). This ensures that the returned reference is valid as long as the input references are valid.

2. Function Signatures with Lifetimes

Lifetimes are especially useful when dealing with function signatures where references are passed around. When multiple references are involved, the compiler needs to know how long each reference is valid.

For example, let's say you have a function that accepts two references and returns one:

rust

```rust
fn first_word(s: &str) -> &str {
    let bytes = s.as_bytes();
    for (i, &item) in bytes.iter().enumerate() {
        if item == b' ' {
            return &s[0..i];
        }
    }
    &s[0..]
}
```

This code won't compile because the return reference `&s[0..i]` may not be valid once the function ends, as `s` is a local variable. The compiler needs to know how long `s` is valid in relation to the returned reference, and this is managed through lifetime annotations.

3. Lifetime Annotations in Structs

Lifetimes are also used in structs to specify how long the data held by the struct is valid. Here's an example of a struct with a lifetime annotation:

rust

```rust
struct Book<'a> {
    title: &'a str,
    author: &'a str,
}
```

In this case, both `title` and `author` references must live at least as long as the lifetime `'a` for the `Book` struct to be valid. This ensures that the data inside the struct doesn't become invalid while the struct is still in use.

Hands-on Project: Build a Memory-Intensive Application and Explain How the Memory Model Works

Let's apply the concepts we've discussed by building a memory-intensive application. In this project, we'll create a simple program that processes a large collection of data, using both heap and stack memory. We'll also explore how ownership, borrowing, and lifetime annotations work in real-world scenarios.

For this hands-on project, we'll build an application that simulates processing a list of large strings by performing several transformations on them concurrently. The program will allocate data on the heap, and we'll demonstrate how to manage it using Rust's memory model.

```rust
rust

use std::thread;
use std::sync::{Arc, Mutex};
```

```rust
fn process_data(data: &str) -> String {
    // Simulate a computation-heavy task
    let mut result = data.to_string();
    result.push_str(" processed!");
    result
}

fn main() {
    let data = Arc::new(Mutex::new(vec![
        String::from("data1"),
        String::from("data2"),
        String::from("data3"),
    ]));

    let mut handles = vec![];

    for _ in 0..3 {
        let data_clone = Arc::clone(&data);

        let handle = thread::spawn(move || {
            let mut data =
data_clone.lock().unwrap();
            let processed_data =
data.iter_mut().map(|item|
process_data(item)).collect::<Vec<_>>();
            println!("{:?}", processed_data);
        });

        handles.push(handle);
```

```
    }

    for handle in handles {
        handle.join().unwrap();
    }
}
```

What's Happening in the Code?

1. **Heap and Stack Memory**:
   - The `data` variable is allocated on the heap, as it is a `Vec<String>`, and it's shared across multiple threads using `Arc` (Atomic Reference Counting).
   - `Arc` allows us to safely share ownership of `data` across threads, while `Mutex` ensures that only one thread can mutate the data at a time.

2. **Concurrency**:
   - We spawn three threads, each of which processes the data concurrently. Each thread locks the data, processes it, and prints the result.

3. **Borrowing and Ownership**:
   - The use of `Arc<Mutex<T>>` ensures that each thread has access to the data safely. The `Mutex` ensures that only one thread can modify the data at a time, preventing data races.

4. **Lifetime Annotations**:

○ In this case, the lifetime of the data is managed implicitly by `Arc` and `Mutex`. Rust's ownership and borrowing rules ensure that the memory is valid for as long as it's being used, and no references outlive their data.

Conclusion

Rust's memory management model is one of its most powerful features. By leveraging concepts like stack and heap memory, the borrow checker, and lifetime annotations, Rust ensures that your programs are both memory-efficient and free from common bugs like dangling pointers and data races. This chapter has provided an in-depth understanding of how Rust manages memory at both the low and high levels, and we've seen how the ownership model applies to different types of memory allocation.

The hands-on project allowed us to see how these concepts come together in a real-world application, demonstrating the safety and power of Rust's memory management. As you continue working with Rust, these principles will be crucial for writing efficient, safe, and reliable programs, particularly in systems programming and multithreaded applications.

Chapter 9: Working with External Libraries in Rust

Using Crates: How to Use External Libraries in Rust via Cargo

Rust has a rich ecosystem of external libraries, known as **crates**, that can be easily integrated into your projects. A crate can be thought of as a package of Rust code that you can use in your own programs. Using external libraries in Rust is straightforward thanks to the package manager and build tool **Cargo**, which comes with Rust by default.

Cargo is the official Rust tool used for managing dependencies, compiling your projects, and running tests. It is designed to make it easy to fetch, build, and manage Rust libraries from the central repository, **crates.io**, which is where all public crates are stored.

1. Adding Crates to Your Project

When you want to use an external crate, you first need to add it to your project's `Cargo.toml` file. This file acts as the configuration file for your project and lists the dependencies, among other things. To use a crate, you just need to specify its name and version in the `[dependencies]` section of `Cargo.toml`.

For example, if you want to use the **serde** crate for serializing and deserializing data, you would add it like this:

toml

```
[dependencies]
serde = "1.0"
serde_json = "1.0"
```

Once you've added the crate to `Cargo.toml`, Cargo will automatically download and compile the crate when you run the project.

2. Fetching and Compiling Crates

After adding a crate to the `Cargo.toml`, you can use Cargo to fetch the crate and its dependencies. This is done by running:

bash

```
cargo build
```

This command will:

1. Download the specified crates and their dependencies from `crates.io`.
2. Compile them into your project.
3. Make them available for use in your Rust code.

You can also fetch and compile the crates in one step by running:

bash

```
cargo run
```

This command will compile your project (if needed) and then run the resulting binary.

3. Using the Crate in Your Code

After adding a crate to your `Cargo.toml`, you can start using it in your code by bringing it into scope with the `use` keyword. For example, using `serde` to serialize and deserialize JSON data:

rust

```rust
use serde::{Serialize, Deserialize};
use serde_json;

#[derive(Serialize, Deserialize)]
struct Person {
    name: String,
    age: u32,
}

fn main() {
    let person = Person {
        name: String::from("Alice"),
        age: 30,
    };

    // Serialize the person object to a JSON string
    let json =
serde_json::to_string(&person).unwrap();
    println!("Serialized: {}", json);
```

```
    // Deserialize the JSON string back to a Person
object
    let deserialized: Person =
serde_json::from_str(&json).unwrap();
    println!("Deserialized: {} is {} years old.",
deserialized.name, deserialized.age);
}
```

In this example:

- We've added the `serde` and `serde_json` crates to `Cargo.toml` and brought them into scope with `use`.
- The `Person` struct is annotated with `#[derive(Serialize, Deserialize)]` to make it serializable and deserializable.
- We serialize a `Person` object to a JSON string and then deserialize it back to a `Person` object.

4. Updating Crates

Crates often receive updates, and Cargo makes it easy to update them to the latest versions. To update a crate, you can modify its version in `Cargo.toml` and run:

bash

```
cargo update
```

This will fetch the latest compatible versions of the crates specified in your `Cargo.toml`.

Creating Your Own Crates: Writing Reusable Libraries in Rust

Rust's design encourages modular code, and crates are one of the best ways to structure and reuse code. Writing your own crates allows you to share functionality between multiple projects, maintain a clean and organized codebase, and reuse code that you or others have written.

1. Creating a New Crate

To create a new crate in Rust, you can use the `cargo new` command. This command creates a new project with the necessary folder structure and files to get started. By default, `cargo new` creates a binary crate (an executable), but you can create a library crate as well.

To create a new library crate:

```bash

cargo new my_library --lib
```

This will create the following structure:

```css
css
```

```
my_library/
    ├── src/
    │   └── lib.rs
    └── Cargo.toml
```

The `lib.rs` file is where you will write the code for your library. The `Cargo.toml` file is where you can configure metadata about the crate, such as its name, version, and dependencies.

2. Writing Library Code

A crate in Rust is essentially a collection of functions, types, and modules. You can define any number of public (`pub`) functions, structs, and other items that can be accessed from outside the crate. For example, you might create a simple library for performing basic arithmetic operations:

```rust
rust

// src/lib.rs

pub fn add(x: i32, y: i32) -> i32 {
    x + y
}

pub fn multiply(x: i32, y: i32) -> i32 {
    x * y
```

```
}
```

In this code:

- We've defined two functions, `add` and `multiply`, both of which are `pub` so they can be accessed from outside the crate.

3. Using Your Library in Another Project

Once you have your library crate, you can include it in another project. If the library is local (i.e., not published to `crates.io`), you can include it in your `Cargo.toml` as a path dependency:

```toml
[dependencies]
my_library = { path = "../my_library" }
```

In this example, `my_library` is located in the directory one level up from the current project.

You can then use the crate like any other external crate:

```rust
use my_library::{add, multiply};

fn main() {
```

```
let sum = add(5, 3);
let product = multiply(5, 3);
println!("Sum: {}, Product: {}", sum, product);
}
```

4. Publishing Your Crate

Once your crate is ready and tested, you can share it with the Rust community by publishing it to **crates.io**, Rust's public package registry. To do this, you'll need a `crates.io` account.

To publish your crate:

1. First, ensure your `Cargo.toml` file is properly configured, including a version number, a description, and the license under which your crate is distributed.

2. Run the following command to log in to `crates.io`:

   bash

   ```
   cargo login
   ```

3. After logging in, publish your crate:

   bash

   ```
   cargo publish
   ```

Once your crate is published, it will be available to anyone who wants to use it via Cargo.

Popular Rust Libraries: An Overview of Commonly Used Rust Crates

Rust has a thriving ecosystem of crates that can help you solve common problems, from web development to data manipulation, and beyond. Here are some of the most popular and useful crates in the Rust ecosystem:

1. Serde (Serialization/Deserialization)

Serde is the most widely used crate for serializing and deserializing data in Rust. It supports a wide range of data formats, including JSON, TOML, and YAML.

```toml
[dependencies]
serde = "1.0"
serde_json = "1.0"
```

Serde's flexibility and performance make it the go-to crate for working with data formats in Rust.

2. Tokio (Asynchronous Programming)

Tokio is the asynchronous runtime for Rust. It enables you to write high-performance, asynchronous programs and works well with Rust's async/await syntax.

```toml
[dependencies]
tokio = { version = "1", features = ["full"] }
```

Tokio powers many Rust web servers and other I/O-bound applications by enabling efficient asynchronous I/O.

3. Rayon (Parallelism)

Rayon is a data parallelism library for Rust. It simplifies parallel processing of data, allowing you to parallelize tasks such as iterating over vectors or arrays with minimal effort.

```toml
[dependencies]
rayon = "1.5"
```

Rayon is perfect for CPU-bound tasks where you need to process large amounts of data concurrently without worrying about managing threads manually.

4. Reqwest (HTTP Client)

Reqwest is a simple and powerful HTTP client for Rust, built on top of the `hyper` library. It allows you to send HTTP requests and handle responses in a way that is easy to use.

```toml
[dependencies]
reqwest = { version = "0.11", features = ["json"] }
```

Reqwest is commonly used for making web requests in Rust, whether for REST APIs or other HTTP-based services.

Hands-on Project: Build an Application Using Multiple Crates and Demonstrate How to Organize Them

For this project, we'll build a simple command-line application that fetches data from an external API, processes it, and displays the results. We'll use several crates to handle different parts of the process:

1. **Reqwest** to fetch data from the API.
2. **Serde** to deserialize the data.
3. **Clap** to parse command-line arguments.

Let's build the app step-by-step.

1. Setting Up Dependencies

Start by creating a new project:

```bash
cargo new weather_app --bin
```

Then, add the following dependencies to `Cargo.toml`:

```toml
[dependencies]
reqwest = { version = "0.11", features = ["json"] }
serde = "1.0"
serde_json = "1.0"
clap = "3.0"
tokio = { version = "1", features = ["full"] }
```

2. Fetching Data with Reqwest

We'll use the **OpenWeatherMap API** to fetch weather data. First, we need to make a request to their API. To do this, we'll create an asynchronous function that fetches the data using `reqwest`.

```rust
use reqwest::Error;
```

```rust
use serde::{Deserialize, Serialize};

#[derive(Serialize, Deserialize, Debug)]
struct Weather {
    main: Main,
}

#[derive(Serialize, Deserialize, Debug)]
struct Main {
    temp: f64,
}

async fn get_weather(city: &str) -> Result<f64,
Error> {
    let api_key = "your_api_key";
    let url = format!(

"http://api.openweathermap.org/data/2.5/weather?q={}&
appid={}&units=metric",
        city, api_key
    );

    let response =
reqwest::get(&url).await?.json::<Weather>().await?;
    Ok(response.main.temp)
}
```

In this code:

- We define `Weather` and `Main` structs to match the JSON response structure from the OpenWeatherMap API.
- The `get_weather` function makes an asynchronous GET request to fetch the weather data for a given city.

3. Processing and Displaying Data

Now, we need to process the data and display the temperature to the user. We'll use the **Clap** crate to handle command-line arguments:

```rust
use clap::{App, Arg};

#[tokio::main]
async fn main() {
    let matches = App::new("Weather App")
        .version("1.0")
        .author("Your Name")
        .about("Fetches weather data for a given
city")
        .arg(
            Arg::new("city")
                .about("The city to get weather data
for")
                .required(true)
                .index(1),
        )
        .get_matches();
```

```
let city = matches.value_of("city").unwrap();
match get_weather(city).await {
    Ok(temp) => println!("The temperature in {}
is {:.2}°C", city, temp),
    Err(e) => eprintln!("Error fetching weather
data: {}", e),
}
}
```

4. Running the Application

To run the application, use the following command:

```bash
cargo run -- "London"
```

This will fetch the weather data for **London** and display the temperature.

Conclusion

In this chapter, we've explored how to work with external libraries in Rust using **Cargo**, the tool that makes managing dependencies and building projects a breeze. We've learned how to add external crates to your projects, how to write reusable libraries, and how to structure and publish your own crates.

We also took a hands-on approach, building a simple command-line application that fetches weather data using **Reqwest**, processes it with **Serde**, and interacts with the user via **Clap**.

Rust's ecosystem is rich with high-quality crates that make it easy to solve real-world problems. Whether you're building web servers, working with databases, or handling I/O-bound tasks, Rust has a crate for you. By mastering how to use and create crates, you'll be able to tackle a wide variety of tasks in your own projects.

Chapter 10: Building Scalable Applications with Microservices

Microservices Architecture Basics: Understanding Microservices and How Rust Fits In

Microservices architecture is a way of designing and building software applications that are structured as a collection of loosely coupled services. Each service represents a distinct business capability, running independently and communicating with other services via well-defined interfaces, typically over HTTP/REST or messaging queues. This architectural style contrasts with monolithic systems, where all components are tightly integrated into a single unit.

The core idea behind microservices is to break down complex applications into smaller, manageable, and independently deployable pieces. This approach provides several benefits:

- **Scalability**: Each service can be scaled independently based on its resource requirements.
- **Flexibility**: Developers can choose different technologies for different services based on their specific needs.

- **Resilience**: If one service fails, it doesn't necessarily bring down the entire application, as services are isolated from each other.
- **Faster Development**: Teams can develop and deploy services independently, speeding up the development cycle.

Rust is an excellent fit for building microservices for several reasons. It combines performance and memory safety with a modern programming paradigm, making it well-suited for systems programming where efficiency and concurrency are important. Additionally, Rust's compile-time checks ensure that microservices are reliable from the get-go, reducing runtime errors and improving the stability of the system.

In this chapter, we'll explore how to design and build microservices in Rust, with a particular focus on building scalable, reliable systems. We'll cover everything from setting up REST APIs to ensuring the application can scale and tolerate faults.

1. Microservices in Practice

A typical microservices-based application might involve the following components:

- **User Authentication**: A service dedicated to handling login, registration, and token management.

- **Product Catalog**: A service that manages product data.
- **Order Management**: A service that handles customer orders.
- **Payment**: A service responsible for payment processing.
- **Inventory**: A service that manages product stock levels.

Each of these services operates independently, often communicating via RESTful APIs or event-driven systems like message queues or Kafka. In a production system, these services would be containerized (using Docker, for example) and orchestrated using Kubernetes or a similar tool.

Building Microservices in Rust: Setting Up REST APIs and Inter-Service Communication

In Rust, building a microservice typically involves setting up a REST API to allow other services or clients to interact with the service. We'll walk through how to set up a basic REST API and ensure that our microservice can communicate effectively with others.

1. Setting Up a REST API with Actix-Web

Rust offers several web frameworks for building RESTful APIs, with **Actix-Web** being one of the most popular choices for its speed and flexibility. Actix-Web provides an easy-to-use and high-performance way to build asynchronous web servers.

To get started, you'll need to add `actix-web` to your `Cargo.toml` file:

```toml
[dependencies]
actix-web = "4.0"
serde = "1.0"
serde_json = "1.0"
```

2. Creating a Basic REST API with Actix-Web

First, let's build a simple REST API that exposes an endpoint for user authentication. We'll handle user login with a simple username/password mechanism.

```rust
use actix_web::{web, App, HttpServer, HttpResponse,
Responder};
use serde::{Deserialize, Serialize};

#[derive(Deserialize)]
struct LoginInfo {
    username: String,
    password: String,
}

#[derive(Serialize)]
struct AuthResponse {
```

```rust
    message: String,
    token: Option<String>,
}


async fn login(info: web::Json<LoginInfo>) -> impl
Responder {
    if info.username == "admin" && info.password ==
"password" {
        let response = AuthResponse {
            message: "Login successful".to_string(),
            token: Some("JWT_TOKEN".to_string()),
        };
        HttpResponse::Ok().json(response)
    } else {

HttpResponse::Unauthorized().json(AuthResponse {
            message: "Invalid
credentials".to_string(),
            token: None,
        })
    }
}


#[actix_web::main]
async fn main() -> std::io::Result<()> {
    HttpServer::new(|| {
        App::new()
            .route("/login", web::post().to(login))
    })
```

```
    .bind("127.0.0.1:8080")?
    .run()
    .await
}
```

In this example:

- We define a `LoginInfo` struct to accept JSON input for the username and password.
- The `login` function checks if the credentials are valid, and returns a JSON response with a message and a token if successful.
- The `AuthResponse` struct is used to structure the JSON response.

To test this API, run the server with `cargo run` and send a POST request to `http://127.0.0.1:8080/login` with JSON data, like so:

json

```
{
  "username": "admin",
  "password": "password"
}
```

You'll get a response with a success message and a token.

3. Inter-Service Communication with HTTP

In a microservices architecture, services often need to communicate with each other. Typically, this is done over HTTP (using REST APIs), but other methods like gRPC or message queues might be used depending on the specific use case.

To send HTTP requests from one Rust service to another, we can use the reqwest crate, which provides a simple interface for making HTTP requests.

Here's an example where the authentication service sends a request to a user data service to fetch additional information about a user after a successful login:

toml

```toml
[dependencies]
reqwest = { version = "0.11", features = ["json"] }
tokio = { version = "1", features = ["full"] }
```

rust

```rust
use reqwest::Client;
use serde::{Deserialize, Serialize};

#[derive(Deserialize, Serialize)]
struct UserData {
    username: String,
```

```
    email: String,
}

async fn fetch_user_data(username: &str) ->
Result<UserData, reqwest::Error> {
    let client = Client::new();
    let url =
format!("http://localhost:8081/users/{}", username);
    let res = client.get(url).send().await?;

    if res.status().is_success() {
        let user_data =
res.json::<UserData>().await?;
        Ok(user_data)
    } else {

Err(reqwest::Error::new(reqwest::StatusCode::BAD_REQU
EST, "Failed to fetch user data"))
    }
}
```

In this example:

- We use `reqwest::Client` to send a `GET` request to another service that provides user data.
- The `fetch_user_data` function retrieves the user's data from the specified service and returns it as a `UserData` struct.

4. Asynchronous Programming with Actix and Reqwest

Rust's async/await syntax allows for efficient, non-blocking I/O operations. Both Actix-Web and Reqwest are designed with async in mind, ensuring that they handle requests and responses in an efficient manner. This is crucial for microservices, where services might have high concurrency and need to handle multiple requests simultaneously.

In the example above, both the REST API and the HTTP requests are asynchronous, allowing multiple requests to be handled concurrently without blocking the execution of other tasks.

Designing for Scalability: Architecting for Reliability, Scaling, and Fault Tolerance

In a microservices architecture, scalability and fault tolerance are critical considerations. Microservices need to be able to handle increased load as the number of users or requests grows, and they must be resilient to failures. Rust's concurrency model, along with its strong type safety and memory management features, makes it well-suited to building scalable and reliable systems.

1. Scalability

Scalability refers to the ability of a system to handle growing amounts of work. In a microservices architecture, scalability can be achieved by:

- **Horizontal Scaling**: Adding more instances of a service to handle increased traffic.
- **Vertical Scaling**: Increasing the resources (CPU, memory) available to a single service instance.

Rust's memory safety and concurrency features help in managing resources efficiently, ensuring that each service can scale independently without running into issues like race conditions or memory leaks.

To scale the authentication service, you could deploy multiple instances of the service behind a load balancer. The load balancer will distribute incoming requests evenly across the instances, improving the service's throughput and resilience.

2. Fault Tolerance

Fault tolerance means the system's ability to continue functioning even if one or more components fail. In a microservices system, fault tolerance is usually achieved by:

- **Replication**: Running multiple instances of a service to ensure that if one instance fails, others can take over.
- **Circuit Breakers**: Automatically handling failures by stopping requests to a failing service until it recovers.

Rust's ownership and borrowing model make it easy to reason about memory and concurrency, which is crucial in building systems that can withstand failures.

3. Designing for Reliability

Reliability is about ensuring the system behaves as expected, even when it faces edge cases or failures. When building microservices in Rust, reliability can be achieved by:

- **Testing**: Writing unit tests, integration tests, and end-to-end tests to ensure that each service behaves as expected under normal and abnormal conditions.
- **Graceful Degradation**: Ensuring that when a service fails, the system continues to function in a degraded but acceptable state, rather than completely failing.

In Rust, the strong type system and borrow checker help eliminate many potential runtime errors, ensuring that services are more reliable and less prone to memory-related bugs.

Hands-on Project: Create a Simple Microservice with Rust That Handles User Authentication

In this hands-on project, we will build a simple user authentication service using Rust and the Actix-Web framework. This service will handle user login, validate credentials, and provide an authentication token.

1. Setting Up Dependencies

First, we need to set up the `Cargo.toml` file to include the necessary dependencies:

toml

```toml
[dependencies]
actix-web = "4.0"
serde = "1.0"
serde_json = "1.0"
jsonwebtoken = "7.2"
dotenv = "0.15"
```

- `actix-web` will allow us to build the web service.
- `serde` and `serde_json` will help us handle JSON serialization and deserialization.
- `jsonwebtoken` will allow us to issue and verify JWT tokens.

- dotenv will be used to load environment variables, such as secret keys for JWTs.

2. Creating the Service

Now, let's build the authentication service:

rust

```rust
use actix_web::{web, App, HttpServer, HttpResponse, Responder};
use serde::{Deserialize, Serialize};
use jsonwebtoken::{encode, Header, EncodingKey, decode, DecodingKey, Validation};
use std::env;

#[derive(Deserialize)]
struct LoginInfo {
    username: String,
    password: String,
}

#[derive(Serialize)]
struct AuthResponse {
    message: String,
    token: Option<String>,
}

#[derive(Debug, Deserialize)]
```

```rust
struct Claims {
    sub: String,
    exp: usize,
}


async fn login(info: web::Json<LoginInfo>) -> impl
Responder {
    if info.username == "admin" && info.password ==
"password" {
        let my_claims = Claims {
            sub: "admin".to_owned(),
            exp: 10000000000
        };
        let secret_key =
env::var("JWT_SECRET_KEY").expect("JWT_SECRET_KEY
must be set");

        let token = encode(&Header::default(),
&my_claims,
&EncodingKey::from_secret(secret_key.as_ref()))
            .unwrap();

        let response = AuthResponse {
            message: "Login successful".to_string(),
            token: Some(token),
        };
        HttpResponse::Ok().json(response)
    } else {
```

```
HttpResponse::Unauthorized().json(AuthResponse {
            message: "Invalid
credentials".to_string(),
            token: None,
        })
    }
}


#[actix_web::main]
async fn main() -> std::io::Result<()> {
    dotenv::dotenv().ok();

    HttpServer::new(|| {
        App::new()
            .route("/login", web::post().to(login))
    })
    .bind("127.0.0.1:8080")?
    .run()
    .await
}
```

3. Testing the Microservice

To test the microservice, we'll send a POST request to the `/login`
endpoint with a username and password. If the credentials are
correct, the service will return a JWT token.

You can use tools like Postman or `curl` to test this service:

```
bash
```

```
curl -X POST http://127.0.0.1:8080/login -d
'{"username":"admin", "password":"password"}' -H
"Content-Type: application/json"
```

If successful, the server will return a JSON response containing the authentication token.

Conclusion

Rust provides a solid foundation for building scalable, reliable, and efficient microservices. Through its powerful concurrency model and memory safety features, Rust enables developers to write high-performance microservices that can scale with ease. By combining Rust's robust web frameworks like **Actix-Web** and its efficient asynchronous model, you can build scalable microservices with strong guarantees against runtime errors and bugs.

In this chapter, we've learned the basics of microservices architecture, how to build microservices in Rust using REST APIs, and how to design for scalability and fault tolerance. We also built a simple authentication microservice and demonstrated how to organize and manage inter-service communication.

As you continue to explore Rust's capabilities, you'll find that it is an excellent choice for building fast, reliable, and scalable microservices that can handle modern workloads with ease.

Chapter 11: Testing and Debugging in Rust

Unit and Integration Tests: Writing Tests in Rust Using the Built-in Test Framework

Testing is a crucial part of software development. It ensures that your code behaves as expected and helps you catch issues early. In Rust, the testing framework is built into the language and is designed to work seamlessly with the language's tooling, like `cargo`. Rust's built-in test framework allows you to write unit tests and integration tests that are both efficient and easy to use.

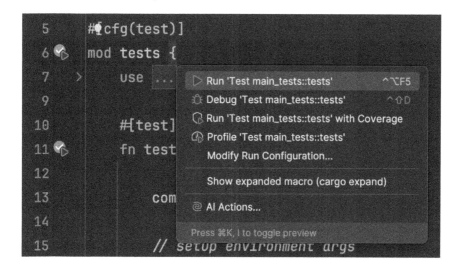

1. Unit Tests in Rust

Unit tests focus on testing small, isolated pieces of functionality, typically functions or methods. Unit tests are essential because they allow you to verify that individual components of your code work correctly in isolation before combining them into larger systems. Rust makes it easy to write unit tests with its built-in test framework.

A basic unit test in Rust is written inside the `tests` module, which is annotated with `#[cfg(test)]` to ensure that it is only compiled and run when testing.

Here's an example of a unit test:

rust

```rust
// Function to test
pub fn add(a: i32, b: i32) -> i32 {
    a + b
}

// Unit test for the add function
#[cfg(test)]
mod tests {
    use super::*;

    #[test]
    fn test_add() {
```

```
        assert eq!(add(2, 3), 5);  // Checks if
add(2, 3) returns 5
        assert_eq!(add(-2, -3), -5);  // Checks if
add(-2, -3) returns -5
    }
}
```

In this example:

- The `add` function is defined to take two integers and return their sum.
- The `#[cfg(test)]` attribute tells the Rust compiler to include the following code only when testing.
- Inside the `tests` module, we define the test function `test_add`. The `#[test]` attribute marks this function as a test.
- The `assert_eq!` macro is used to check that the expected result (the sum of `2 + 3`, which should be `5`) matches the actual result.

2. Running Unit Tests

To run unit tests in Rust, you can simply use the `cargo test` command. This command will automatically discover and run all functions marked with `#[test]` in your project.

bash

```
cargo test
```

Running this will compile your tests and execute them. If all tests pass, you'll see a message like:

```
arduino
```

```
running 1 test
test tests::test_add ... ok
```

If any test fails, Cargo will display detailed information on what went wrong, helping you debug the issue quickly.

3. Integration Tests

Integration tests verify that the different parts of your program work together correctly. These tests often involve testing interactions between multiple modules, functions, or external resources. Unlike unit tests, integration tests usually test the program as a whole.

In Rust, integration tests are placed in the tests directory at the root of the project. This directory is separate from the main codebase and is specifically for testing. Each file in this directory is compiled as a separate crate, allowing you to test your program's integration with other modules or external libraries.

Here's an example of an integration test:

1. **Creating the `tests` Directory:**

   First, create a `tests` directory if it doesn't already exist in your project root:

   ```bash
   mkdir tests
   ```

2. **Writing an Integration Test:**

   Inside the `tests` directory, create a file, for example, `integration_test.rs`, and write your test:

   ```rust
   // tests/integration_test.rs
   use my_project::add;   // Import the function from your main code

   #[test]
   fn test_add_integration() {
       let result = add(5, 5);
       assert_eq!(result, 10);
   }
   ```

In this test:

- We import the `add` function from the main project code (in this case, from `my_project`).
- The `test_add_integration` function tests that the sum of 5 and 5 equals `10`.

4. Running Integration Tests

To run the integration tests, use the same `cargo test` command. Cargo will automatically discover the tests in the `tests` directory and run them.

```bash
cargo test
```

Cargo will run both unit tests and integration tests, showing the results of each.

Debugging Rust Code: Using Rust's Debugging Tools, Such as println! and cargo test

Debugging is an essential skill for any developer. Rust provides several ways to debug your code, from basic tools like `println!` for inspecting values to more advanced tools such as the built-in debugger.

1. Using println! for Debugging

Rust's `println!` macro is a simple but powerful tool for debugging. It allows you to print values to the console at runtime, helping you inspect variables and program flow. While not as sophisticated as a debugger, `println!` is often sufficient for tracking down simple bugs.

Example:

rust

```
fn add(a: i32, b: i32) -> i32 {
    println!("Adding {} and {}", a, b);   // Print the
values being added
    a + b
}
```

In this example:

- The `println!` macro prints the values of a and b every time the add function is called.
- This helps you inspect the values and ensures that the function is receiving the expected inputs.

While `println!` is quick and useful, it can become cumbersome for more complex debugging tasks. That's where other tools come in.

2. Using the Built-in Debugger: `gdb` and `lldb`

Rust is compatible with external debuggers like **gdb** and **lldb**, which allow for more sophisticated inspection and step-through debugging. Rust's built-in tooling and Cargo make it easy to integrate these debuggers into your workflow.

To use these debuggers, you need to compile your code with debugging symbols by running:

bash

```
cargo build --debug
```

This will compile your code with additional information to allow for better debugging. After building the project, you can run the debugger of your choice, for example, `gdb`:

bash

```
gdb target/debug/my_project
```

This starts the debugger, allowing you to inspect variables, set breakpoints, and step through your code. You can also use `lldb` if you're on macOS or prefer it over `gdb`.

3. Using cargo test for Debugging

Rust's built-in test framework (`cargo test`) is also an invaluable tool for debugging. If a unit test or integration test fails, `cargo test` will display the failure, showing where the test failed and what the expected value was compared to the actual value. This can point out errors and guide you toward a solution.

For more advanced testing, you can add custom debugging code inside your tests, using `println!` or other debugging techniques.

4. Using the debug! and trace! Macros

For more advanced logging, you can use libraries like **log** or **env_logger** to generate different levels of logging messages. These macros provide structured logs at various levels of verbosity, from basic debug info to verbose trace output.

toml

```toml
[dependencies]
log = "0.4"
env_logger = "0.9"
rust
```

```rust
use log::{debug, info};

fn main() {
```

```
    env_logger::init();
    debug!("This is a debug message");
    info!("This is an info message");
}
```

To activate logging, set the `RUST_LOG` environment variable:

```
bash
```

```
RUST_LOG=debug cargo run
```

This will show debug messages in your console output, helping you trace issues more easily.

Handling Errors and Logs: Best Practices for Logging and Debugging in Production

When developing Rust applications, particularly in production environments, proper error handling and logging are essential for tracking down issues and maintaining reliability.

1. Error Handling Best Practices

Rust encourages explicit error handling using the `Result` and `Option` types, which require developers to handle errors at compile time. This makes it easier to write reliable, fault-tolerant programs. The key error types in Rust are:

- **Result<T, E>**: Used for functions that can either succeed (`Ok(T)`) or fail (`Err(E)`).
- **Option<T>**: Used when a value is either `Some(T)` or `None`, typically for cases where something might be missing, such as when searching a map.

Best practices:

- Always handle `Result` and `Option` properly.
- Use `.unwrap()` and `.expect()` sparingly, and only when you are sure the result will not be `Err` or `None`. These methods panic when the value is an error, which is not ideal for production code.
- Propagate errors with the `?` operator to return early when an error occurs, making the code more concise and readable.

Example of error propagation:

rust

```
use std::fs::File;
use std::io::{self, Read};

fn read_file(filename: &str) -> Result<String,
io::Error> {
    let mut file = File::open(filename)?;
    let mut contents = String::new();
```

```
    file.read_to_string(&mut contents)?;
    Ok(contents)
}
```

2. Logging in Production

When it comes to logging, especially in production, it's crucial to have detailed and structured logs that can help diagnose issues without adding too much noise. Use the `log` crate for structured logging at different levels, such as `debug`, `info`, `warn`, `error`, and `trace`.

- **debug**: Detailed messages useful for development.
- **info**: General information about the system's state.
- **warn**: Warnings about potential issues.
- **error**: Critical errors that may require attention.

Logging should be appropriately configured to minimize the performance overhead in production. You can configure the verbosity of logs through the `RUST_LOG` environment variable.

```bash
RUST_LOG=info cargo run
```

This configuration will show logs at the `info` level and higher (i.e., `warn` and `error`).

3. Structured Logging with JSON

For systems that require integration with log aggregation tools like
ELK (Elasticsearch, Logstash, Kibana), using structured logs in JSON
format is a common practice. You can use the `serde_json` crate
along with `log` to serialize logs into JSON.

```toml
toml

[dependencies]
serde_json = "1.0"
log = "0.4"
```

```rust
rust

use serde::Serialize;
use log::{info};

#[derive(Serialize)]
struct LogData {
    user_id: u32,
    action: String,
}

fn main() {
    env_logger::init();

    let log_data = LogData {
        user_id: 1234,
        action: String::from("Login"),
```

```
    };

    info!("{}",
serde_json::to_string(&log_data).unwrap());
}
```

This approach allows you to easily query and analyze logs in production environments.

Hands-on Project: Write Unit Tests for a Previously Created Rust Project and Debug It

In this hands-on project, we will take a previously created Rust project, write comprehensive unit tests for its functions, and then debug any issues that arise.

1. **Test the add Function**

Let's start by writing a unit test for a basic function in the project. The add function should add two integers and return the result.

rust

```
// src/lib.rs

pub fn add(a: i32, b: i32) -> i32 {
    a + b
}
```

```
// tests/integration_test.rs
use my_project::add;

#[test]
fn test_add() {
    assert_eq!(add(2, 3), 5);
    assert_eq!(add(-2, 2), 0);
}
```

Here, we created a test for the `add` function, ensuring that it behaves correctly for both positive and negative numbers.

2. **Debugging with `println!`**

If a test fails, we can use `println!` to print intermediate values and better understand what is going wrong:

rust

```
fn add(a: i32, b: i32) -> i32 {
    println!("Adding {} and {}", a, b);
    a + b
}
```

By running `cargo test`, we can inspect the output and confirm if the issue lies with the logic or the inputs.

3. **Handling Errors and Debugging**

As we write unit tests for more complex functionality, such as network requests or database queries, we will need to handle errors more carefully. We can use `Result` to propagate errors and ensure our application can recover gracefully from issues, especially in production environments.

rust

```rust
fn fetch_data(url: &str) -> Result<String,
reqwest::Error> {
    reqwest::blocking::get(url)?.text()
}
```

With this setup, we can test and debug our application more effectively using Rust's built-in tools.

Conclusion

Testing and debugging are crucial aspects of writing reliable software, and Rust provides powerful tools to make these tasks easier and more effective. By using Rust's built-in test framework, you can write both unit and integration tests that verify your code's correctness. Additionally, Rust's debugging tools, including `println!`, `gdb`, and logging frameworks, help you identify and fix issues quickly. When combined with best practices for error handling and logging, these tools make Rust a great choice for building reliable and efficient systems.

Chapter 12: Building Applications with Asynchronous Rust

Introduction to Asynchronous Programming: Why async/await is Essential for High-Performance Applications

Asynchronous programming has become a key technique in developing high-performance, scalable applications. In traditional synchronous programming, each operation, such as reading data from a file or making an HTTP request, blocks the program until the task is completed. This means that while one operation is waiting for a response, the entire program may be idle, wasting precious resources and time.

Asynchronous programming, on the other hand, allows a program to initiate multiple tasks at once, and while one task is waiting (such as waiting for data from the network), other tasks can continue. This is a highly efficient way to handle operations that involve waiting for external resources, like network calls or file I/O, which are common in modern software applications.

Rust's approach to asynchronous programming is based on the **async/await** syntax, which is designed to simplify asynchronous programming while maintaining Rust's safety and performance guarantees. In this chapter, we will explore the essential concepts of asynchronous programming in Rust and how to write asynchronous functions using `async` and `await`.

1. Why Async/Await is Essential for High-Performance Applications

Asynchronous programming is crucial for building applications that need to handle high concurrency, such as web servers, real-time systems, or any application that requires non-blocking I/O. Without async, your program might be spending time waiting for operations like database queries, file operations, or web requests, which results in inefficiency.

In Rust, asynchronous programming helps achieve:

- **Non-blocking I/O**: By using `async` and `await`, you can make I/O operations (like reading from a file or querying a database) non-blocking. This means while waiting for an operation to complete, the program can do other work.
- **Concurrency**: Async programming allows you to run multiple tasks concurrently without the overhead of creating new threads for each task.

- **Performance**: By minimizing wasted time during I/O-bound tasks, your application can handle more tasks with the same resources.

When combined with Rust's focus on memory safety and performance, `async`/`await` is a powerful tool for writing efficient, scalable applications.

Using Async with Rust: Writing Asynchronous Functions and Working with Futures

In Rust, asynchronous functions are written using the `async` keyword, and the result of an asynchronous function is wrapped in a `Future`. A `Future` represents a value that will be available at some point in the future.

1. Writing Asynchronous Functions

An asynchronous function is defined with the `async fn` syntax. It allows the function to return a `Future` instead of a concrete value immediately. When calling an async function, you need to use `.await` to actually execute the function and get the result.

Here's a basic example of an asynchronous function:

```rust
rust

use tokio;

async fn fetch_data() -> String {
    // Simulate an asynchronous operation
    "Data fetched!".to_string()
}

#[tokio::main]
async fn main() {
    let data = fetch_data().await;
    println!("{}", data);
}
```

In this example:

- The `fetch_data` function is declared as `async` and returns a `String`.
- The `main` function is annotated with `#[tokio::main]`, which sets up the asynchronous runtime.
- Inside `main`, we call `fetch_data().await` to actually execute the async function.

The `await` keyword tells the Rust compiler to pause the current function's execution and yield control back to the runtime while waiting for the result of the asynchronous operation. Once the result is available, the function resumes execution with the value returned.

2. Futures in Rust

A **future** represents a value that will be available at some point. When you call an `async` function, Rust returns a `Future` object. However, you cannot directly use the result of a `Future` without awaiting it, as the result is not available immediately.

The `Future` type is an abstract representation of a value that will be computed asynchronously. It's only when you `.await` the future that Rust schedules the execution and allows the result to be used.

Here's an example that explicitly shows how futures work:

rust

```rust
use std::future::Future;
use tokio;

async fn async_operation() -> u32 {
    42
}

fn example() -> impl Future<Output = u32> {
    async_operation()
}

#[tokio::main]
async fn main() {
    let result = example().await;
```

```
    println!("Result: {}", result);
}
```

In this code:

- `async_operation` returns a `Future` that resolves to a `u32`.
- The `example` function returns an `impl Future`, which is a concrete type that implements the `Future` trait.
- In `main`, we `.await` the future returned by `example()`.

3. Async with Libraries

Rust's async ecosystem is built around asynchronous runtimes. The most popular async runtime for Rust is **Tokio**, which is a fast, flexible, and lightweight asynchronous runtime. To use async features, we often rely on the `tokio` crate, which provides utilities like `tokio::main` for managing the runtime and async task scheduling.

You can add `tokio` to your project's dependencies in `Cargo.toml`:

toml

```toml
[dependencies]
tokio = { version = "1", features = ["full"] }
```

Now, we can write asynchronous functions that make use of Tokio's async I/O capabilities.

```rust
rust

use tokio::fs;

async fn read_file() -> Result<String,
std::io::Error> {
    let contents =
fs::read_to_string("example.txt").await?;
    Ok(contents)
}

#[tokio::main]
async fn main() {
    match read_file().await {
        Ok(content) => println!("File contents: {}",
content),
        Err(e) => eprintln!("Error reading file: {}",
e),
    }
}
```

In this example:

- We use `tokio::fs::read_to_string` to asynchronously read a file.
- The `read_file` function is asynchronous and returns a `Future`, which is awaited in `main`.

Concurrency vs. Parallelism: Understanding the Difference and When to Use Them

While **concurrency** and **parallelism** are often used interchangeably, they represent different concepts in computing, especially when dealing with asynchronous programming. Rust's async model is great for concurrency, but it's essential to understand how concurrency differs from parallelism and when to use each.

1. Concurrency: Handling Multiple Tasks Simultaneously

Concurrency is the ability to run multiple tasks or operations at the same time, but not necessarily simultaneously. With concurrency, tasks may be interleaved, meaning the CPU switches between tasks, but they don't all run at once. This is especially useful for I/O-bound operations like reading from a network or a file system, where you can initiate a task, wait for the response, and then move on to other tasks.

In Rust, asynchronous programming allows for concurrency. When you use `async`/`await`, the program doesn't block while waiting for a task to complete; instead, it continues processing other tasks.

2. Parallelism: Performing Multiple Tasks Simultaneously

Parallelism, on the other hand, refers to executing multiple tasks at exactly the same time. Parallelism is beneficial for CPU-bound tasks, such as processing large datasets or running intensive computations. It requires multi-core processors to execute multiple threads simultaneously.

Rust can handle parallelism using threads. The `std::thread` module allows you to spawn threads and execute them concurrently, utilizing multiple CPU cores for parallel execution.

3. Concurrency and Parallelism in Rust

Rust's concurrency model is designed to work with asynchronous tasks without blocking. However, if you need to perform parallel computations, you can use the standard threading model alongside async. For example, you can run asynchronous tasks concurrently, while also running compute-bound tasks in parallel using threads.

Here's an example that uses both concurrency and parallelism in Rust:

rust

```rust
use std::thread;
use tokio;

async fn fetch_data() -> String {
    "Data fetched from the network".to_string()
}
```

```rust
fn compute_heavy_task() -> u64 {
    let mut sum = 0;
    for i in 0..1_000_000 {
        sum += i;
    }
    sum
}


#[tokio::main]
async fn main() {
    let fetch_task = tokio::spawn(async {
        fetch_data().await
    });

    let compute_task = thread::spawn(|| {
        compute_heavy_task()
    });

    let fetch_result = fetch_task.await.unwrap();
    let compute_result =
compute_task.join().unwrap();

    println!("Fetch Result: {}", fetch_result);
    println!("Compute Result: {}", compute_result);
}
```

In this example:

- We use **Tokio** to fetch data asynchronously (`fetch_data`).

- We spawn a thread to run a CPU-bound task (`compute_heavy_task`), making use of parallelism.
- This approach combines both concurrency (non-blocking async I/O) and parallelism (multi-threading for CPU-bound tasks).

Hands-on Project: Build an Asynchronous File Downloader That Fetches Multiple Files Concurrently

In this hands-on project, we will build a file downloader that fetches multiple files concurrently. This will demonstrate how to use asynchronous Rust to handle I/O-bound tasks in parallel, providing a scalable and efficient solution for downloading files from the internet.

1. Setting Up Dependencies

First, we need to add dependencies for asynchronous HTTP requests and file handling. Add the following to your `Cargo.toml`:

toml

```toml
[dependencies]
reqwest = { version = "0.11", features = ["json",
"blocking"] }
tokio = { version = "1", features = ["full"] }
```

```
futures = "0.3"
```

We will use **reqwest** for fetching files asynchronously, and **tokio** for the asynchronous runtime.

2. Creating the Downloader

We will create an asynchronous function that downloads a file from a URL and saves it to the disk.

rust

```rust
use reqwest::Client;
use tokio::fs::File;
use tokio::io::AsyncWriteExt;

async fn download_file(url: &str, filename: &str) ->
Result<(), reqwest::Error> {
    let client = Client::new();
    let mut response = client.get(url).send().await?;

    let mut file = File::create(filename).await?;

    while let Some(chunk) = response.chunk().await? {
        file.write_all(&chunk).await?;
    }

    println!("Downloaded file: {}", filename);
    Ok(())
```

```
}
```

In this code:

- We use `reqwest::Client` to send a GET request and fetch the file.
- The file is written asynchronously using `tokio::fs::File`, and chunks of data are written as they are received.
- The `while let Some(chunk)` loop continues to download the file in chunks until it is fully received.

3. Downloading Multiple Files Concurrently

Now, let's download multiple files concurrently using Rust's async capabilities. We will fetch multiple URLs in parallel, leveraging async to download the files concurrently.

rust

```rust
use futures::future::join_all;

async fn download_files(urls: Vec<&str>) ->
Result<(), reqwest::Error> {
    let mut tasks = Vec::new();

    for (i, url) in urls.iter().enumerate() {
        let filename = format!("file_{}.txt", i + 1);
        tasks.push(download_file(*url, &filename));
```

```
    }

    let results = join_all(tasks).await;

    for result in results {
        result?; // Ensure all downloads are
successful
    }

    Ok(())
}

#[tokio::main]
async fn main() {
    let urls = vec![
        "https://www.example.com/file1.txt",
        "https://www.example.com/file2.txt",
        "https://www.example.com/file3.txt",
    ];

    if let Err(e) = download_files(urls).await {
        eprintln!("Error downloading files: {}", e);
    }
}
```

Here:

- We use `join_all` from the `futures` crate to execute all the download tasks concurrently.

- Each task downloads a file asynchronously, and `join_all` waits for all the tasks to finish.
- Once all downloads are completed, we print the results.

4. Running the Application

To run the application, use the following command:

```bash
bash
```

```bash
cargo run
```

This will download the files concurrently and save them to the local disk.

Conclusion

In this chapter, we've explored asynchronous programming in Rust and demonstrated how to build high-performance applications using async/await. We've learned the fundamental concepts of async programming, how to write asynchronous functions, and how Rust's async model can be used to build scalable applications that handle I/O-bound tasks efficiently.

By combining asynchronous I/O with Rust's powerful concurrency model, we can write programs that are both fast and efficient, handling many tasks concurrently without blocking. In the hands-on project, we demonstrated how to download multiple files concurrently, showcasing how async/await can be used to handle multiple tasks efficiently.

Understanding concurrency vs parallelism and knowing when to use each technique is essential for building scalable applications. Rust's asynchronous programming model, combined with its memory safety guarantees, provides a robust foundation for building high-performance, fault-tolerant systems.

Chapter 13: Rust in the Web: Building Web Servers with Rocket

Introducing Rocket Framework: Setting Up Rocket to Build Fast Web Applications

Rust is a language known for its performance, memory safety, and concurrency capabilities, making it an excellent choice for building high-performance web servers. One of the most popular web frameworks for Rust is **Rocket**, which is known for its ease of use, flexibility, and speed. Rocket allows developers to write fast, secure web applications using Rust's modern tooling and features.

In this chapter, we'll take a deep dive into **Rocket**, a web framework built for rapid development of fast and secure web applications in Rust. We'll explore how to set up Rocket, build RESTful APIs, handle HTTP requests, and deploy Rust-based web applications effectively.

1. What is Rocket?

Rocket is a web framework built on top of Rust that simplifies web application development. It's designed to be easy to use while offering the performance and safety guarantees that Rust is known for. With Rocket, you can easily create HTTP servers, handle requests, route URLs to functions, and manage responses. It abstracts away many complexities of web development while still providing full control over how your web application operates.

Rocket is built on top of Rust's async/await system, making it perfect for handling high levels of concurrent connections efficiently. It also integrates well with Rust's strong type system, ensuring that your code is safe and robust from the start.

2. Why Use Rocket?

Rocket provides several advantages for web development:

- **Ease of Use**: Rocket allows you to quickly define routes, request handlers, and responses with minimal boilerplate. Its declarative routing syntax is easy to understand and use.
- **Performance**: Rocket is built with Rust's performance characteristics in mind, ensuring fast execution times for both synchronous and asynchronous operations.
- **Safety**: Thanks to Rust's ownership model, Rocket provides strong guarantees of memory safety, preventing common web application vulnerabilities like data races and null pointer dereferencing.

- **Extensibility**: Rocket allows you to extend functionality with middleware, making it easy to add features such as authentication, logging, and more.

3. Setting Up Rocket

Before you can start building with Rocket, you need to set up your project and add Rocket as a dependency. To do this, you'll need to add Rocket to your `Cargo.toml` file.

```toml
[dependencies]
rocket = "0.5"
tokio = { version = "1", features = ["full"] }
```

- **Rocket**: The main web framework.
- **Tokio**: Rocket uses `tokio` as an asynchronous runtime, so you need it for handling async tasks.

Once you've added the dependencies, you can start creating your first Rocket web application.

4. Creating a Basic Rocket Web Server

Let's start by building a basic Rocket application. Create a new Rust project:

```bash
bash

cargo new rocket_blog --bin
```

Navigate into the project directory and open the `main.rs` file located in the `src` folder. Replace its contents with the following code to set up a basic web server:

```rust
rust

#[macro_use] extern crate rocket;

#[launch]
fn rocket() -> _ {
    rocket::build().mount("/", routes![index])
}

#[get("/")]
fn index() -> &'static str {
    "Welcome to Rocket!"
}
```

In this example:

- The `#[macro_use]` attribute allows us to use Rocket's macros.

- The `rocket()` function creates the web server and specifies the routes it should use. The `mount()` function maps the route `/` to the `index()` function.
- The `#[get("/")]` macro defines an HTTP GET route that handles requests to the root URL (`/`).

To run the server, use the following command:

```bash
cargo run
```

Once the server is running, open your browser and visit `http://localhost:8000/`. You should see "Welcome to Rocket!" displayed on the page.

Building REST APIs: Understanding How to Create and Handle HTTP Requests in Rocket

One of the most common use cases for Rocket is building RESTful APIs. Rocket's routing system makes it easy to handle different HTTP methods (GET, POST, PUT, DELETE) and map them to the appropriate functions in your application.

1. Handling GET Requests

GET requests are used to retrieve information from the server. Let's modify our basic Rocket application to handle GET requests for fetching a list of blog posts.

```rust
#[macro_use] extern crate rocket;

#[launch]
fn rocket() -> _ {
    rocket::build().mount("/", routes![get_posts])
}

#[derive(Serialize)]
struct Post {
    title: String,
    content: String,
}

#[get("/posts")]
fn get_posts() -> Vec<Post> {
    vec![
        Post {
            title: "Post 1".to_string(),
            content: "This is the first post".to_string(),
        },
```

```
        Post {
            title: "Post 2".to_string(),
            content: "This is the second
post".to_string(),
        },
    ]
}
```

In this code:

- We've defined a `Post` struct that will hold the title and content of each blog post.
- The `get_posts` function handles the GET request to `/posts` and returns a list of `Post` objects.
- The `#[derive(Serialize)]` macro ensures that the `Post` struct can be serialized into JSON.

To enable Rocket to serialize data, add the `serde` and `serde_json` crates to your `Cargo.toml` file:

```toml
[dependencies]
rocket = "0.5"
serde = "1.0"
serde_json = "1.0"
tokio = { version = "1", features = ["full"] }
```

Now, the server will return a list of posts when you visit
`http://localhost:8000/posts`.

2. Handling POST Requests

POST requests are used to send data to the server, often for creating
new resources. Let's add a POST endpoint that allows users to
create new blog posts.

rust

```rust
#[macro_use] extern crate rocket;

use rocket::serde::{json::Json, Deserialize};

#[launch]
fn rocket() -> _ {
    rocket::build().mount("/", routes![create_post])
}

#[derive(Deserialize)]
struct NewPost {
    title: String,
    content: String,
}

#[post("/posts", format = "json", data =
"<new_post>")]
fn create_post(new_post: Json<NewPost>) -> String {
```

```
    format!("New post created: {}", new_post.title)
}
```

In this code:

- We've added a `NewPost` struct that represents the data we'll receive in the POST request.
- The `#[derive(Deserialize)]` macro allows Rocket to deserialize the incoming JSON data into the `NewPost` struct.
- The `create_post` function handles POST requests to `/posts`. It takes a `Json<NewPost>` parameter, which is Rocket's way of handling incoming JSON data.

To test this, you can send a POST request to `http://localhost:8000/posts` with JSON data:

```json
{
    "title": "New Post",
    "content": "This is a new blog post."
}
```

3. Handling PUT and DELETE Requests

The same principles apply for handling PUT (for updating resources) and DELETE (for removing resources) requests. Here's an example of how you might implement PUT and DELETE endpoints for a blog API:

```
rust

#[put("/posts/<id>", format = "json", data =
"<updated_post>")]
fn update_post(id: usize, updated_post:
Json<NewPost>) -> String {
    format!("Post {} updated: {}", id,
updated_post.title)
}

#[delete("/posts/<id>")]
fn delete_post(id: usize) -> String {
    format!("Post {} deleted", id)
}
```

In these examples:

- The `update_post` function handles PUT requests to update an existing post.
- The `delete_post` function handles DELETE requests to remove a post.

Deploying Rust Web Apps: Best Practices for Deploying Rust-Based Web Servers

Once your Rust-based web application is ready, the next step is deploying it to a production environment. Deploying a Rust web app comes with its own set of challenges, such as ensuring the app runs efficiently, handling scaling, and managing dependencies.

1. Building a Release Version

Before deploying, you'll want to build a release version of your Rust app. By default, Cargo builds your app in debug mode, which is optimized for development and debugging, but not for performance. To build a release version, use the following command:

```bash
cargo build --release
```

This will compile your project with optimizations, ensuring better performance in a production environment.

2. Deploying with Docker

Docker is a popular way to deploy applications because it allows you to package your app along with its dependencies into a portable container. Here's how to deploy your Rocket application using Docker.

- **Step 1**: Create a `Dockerfile` in the root of your project:

```Dockerfile
FROM rust:1.56 as builder
```

```
WORKDIR /app
 . .
RUN cargo build --release

FROM debian:buster-slim
WORKDIR /app
 --from=builder /app/target/release/rocket_blog .
CMD ["./rocket_blog"]
```

- **Step 2**: Build the Docker image:

bash

```
docker build -t rocket_blog .
```

- **Step 3**: Run the container:

bash

```
docker run -p 8000:8000 rocket_blog
```

This will package your Rust web application into a Docker container, and you can now run it on any system that supports Docker.

3. Scaling Your Application

To handle increased traffic, you can scale your Rust web application horizontally by running multiple instances behind a load balancer. In production environments, you can use tools like **Kubernetes** to manage these instances, ensuring that your application scales automatically as demand increases.

4. Handling Configuration and Secrets

In production, you will need to manage sensitive data like database connection strings, API keys, and other secrets. A common approach is to use environment variables or a secrets manager to handle this data securely. Rocket provides a simple way to load environment variables using the `dotenv` crate.

Here's how to load a secret key from an environment file:

```toml
[dependencies]
dotenv = "0.15"
```

```rust
use dotenv::dotenv;
use std::env;

#[launch]
fn rocket() -> _ {
    dotenv().ok();
    let secret_key =
env::var("SECRET_KEY").expect("SECRET_KEY must be
set");
    rocket::build()
```

```
}
```

In this code, the `dotenv` crate loads the environment variables from a `.env` file, allowing you to securely access secret values like API keys and database credentials.

Hands-on Project: Develop a Simple Blog Application Using Rocket

Let's put everything we've learned into practice by building a simple blog application using Rocket. Our blog will have features for:

1. Viewing a list of blog posts.
2. Creating new posts.
3. Updating existing posts.
4. Deleting posts.

1. Setting Up the Project

Create a new project:

bash

```
cargo new rocket_blog --bin
```

Add the necessary dependencies to your `Cargo.toml`:

```toml
toml

[dependencies]
rocket = "0.5"
serde = "1.0"
serde_json = "1.0"
tokio = { version = "1", features = ["full"] }
```

2. Creating the Blog Application

In the `src/main.rs` file, we will define our blog posts and implement routes for creating, viewing, updating, and deleting posts.

```rust
rust

use rocket::{get, post, put, delete, routes};
use rocket::serde::{Deserialize, Serialize};

#[derive(Serialize, Deserialize, Clone)]
struct Post {
    id: usize,
    title: String,
    content: String,
}

#[get("/posts")]
fn get_posts() -> Vec<Post> {
    vec![
```

```
        Post { id: 1, title: "First
Post".to_string(), content: "This is the first
post.".to_string() },
        Post { id: 2, title: "Second
Post".to_string(), content: "This is the second
post.".to_string() },
    ]
}


#[post("/posts", format = "json", data =
"<new_post>")]
fn create_post(new_post:
rocket::serde::json::Json<Post>) -> String {
    format!("New post created with title: {}",
new_post.title)
}


#[put("/posts/<id>", format = "json", data =
"<updated_post>")]
fn update_post(id: usize, updated_post:
rocket::serde::json::Json<Post>) -> String {
    format!("Post {} updated with title: {}", id,
updated_post.title)
}


#[delete("/posts/<id>")]
fn delete_post(id: usize) -> String {
    format!("Post {} deleted", id)
}
```

```
#[launch]
fn rocket() -> _ {
    rocket::build().mount("/", routes![get_posts,
create_post, update_post, delete_post])
}
```

3. Running the Application

To run the application, execute:

```bash
```

```
cargo run
```

Visit `http://localhost:8000/posts` to see the list of posts, and use a tool like Postman to test the POST, PUT, and DELETE endpoints.

Conclusion

In this chapter, we've explored how to build web applications with Rocket, a powerful web framework for Rust. We've learned how to set up Rocket, build RESTful APIs, and handle HTTP requests such as GET, POST, PUT, and DELETE. Additionally, we covered best practices for deploying Rust-based web servers, including Docker and environment variable management.

In the hands-on project, we developed a simple blog application with Rocket, demonstrating how easy it is to build web applications in Rust with Rocket's powerful routing, serialization, and request handling features. Rocket's combination of performance, safety, and ease of use makes it an excellent choice for web development in Rust. Whether you are building a small API or a full-scale web application, Rocket provides the tools you need to build fast, secure, and scalable systems.

Chapter 14: Rust for Embedded Systems

What is Embedded Systems Programming?: Overview of Embedded Programming with Rust

Embedded systems programming refers to the process of writing software that directly interacts with hardware. These systems are typically designed for specific tasks and have constraints such as limited processing power, memory, and power availability. Examples of embedded systems include microcontrollers in devices like smart thermostats, washing machines, and medical equipment, as well as more complex systems such as automotive control systems or industrial automation systems.

Programming embedded systems requires an understanding of both software and hardware, along with the constraints of the environment. In traditional software development, applications run on high-powered devices with rich operating systems, but embedded systems are often resource-constrained and do not have the luxury of such environments. Instead, the program must interact directly with the hardware to achieve desired results.

Rust has increasingly become a go-to language for embedded systems programming because of its unique combination of performance, safety, and control over hardware. Rust ensures memory safety through its ownership model without sacrificing performance, which is critical in embedded systems where every byte and CPU cycle counts. Moreover, Rust's rich type system prevents bugs during compile-time, making it a perfect choice for embedded systems that require high reliability.

In this chapter, we will dive into how to use Rust for embedded systems, set up the development environment, and integrate Rust with real-time operating systems (RTOS) for performance-critical applications.

Setting Up Embedded Development Environments: Tools and Platforms Used in Embedded Rust Programming

Setting up the development environment for embedded Rust is not as straightforward as standard Rust development, primarily because embedded programming involves low-level hardware interactions and often requires cross-compilation for target platforms. However, Rust has an active ecosystem and well-maintained tools that make the process much smoother.

1. Choosing a Platform and Microcontroller

The first step in embedded development is to choose a platform or microcontroller. Rust can be used to program a wide range of embedded devices, from simple microcontrollers like the **Arduino** or **Raspberry Pi Pico** to more complex, resource-rich devices.

- **Arduino**: One of the most well-known microcontroller platforms, Arduino offers an extensive range of devices from basic to more complex boards. Rust is supported on many Arduino boards, such as the Arduino Uno, via cross-compilation.
- **Raspberry Pi Pico**: The Raspberry Pi Pico is based on the RP2040 microcontroller and is a great platform for learning embedded development with Rust. The `rp-hal` crate provides support for programming the RP2040 with Rust.
- **STM32**: For more performance-critical applications, STM32 microcontrollers are widely used in the industry, and Rust has excellent support for this platform through crates like `stm32-hal`.

2. Setting Up Cross-Compilation for Embedded Rust

Cross-compilation is the process of compiling software on one architecture (such as an x86 PC) for another architecture (such as an ARM-based microcontroller). Rust provides strong support for cross-compilation via the rustup tool, which simplifies the setup of cross-compilation targets.

To get started with cross-compiling for embedded systems, follow these steps:

1. **Install Rust for the Target Architecture**: First, you'll need to install the appropriate toolchain for your target architecture. For example, for ARM-based devices like the Raspberry Pi Pico, you would add the ARM target using the following command:

    bash

    ```
    rustup target add thumbv6m-none-eabi
    ```

2. **Install the Required Toolchain**: Next, you'll need to install the toolchain for compiling code for your embedded platform. This usually involves installing `arm-none-eabi-gcc` or a similar tool for your architecture. On a Linux system, you can install it using:

    bash

    ```
    sudo apt install gcc-arm-none-eabi
    ```

3. **Setting Up Cargo for Cross-Compilation**: Use `cargo` to build and run code for embedded targets. You can configure your `Cargo.toml` and `Cargo.config` to specify the target architecture and toolchain.

4. **Flashing to the Device**: After building your application, the next step is flashing it to the target microcontroller. Tools like `OpenOCD` and `cargo-flash` can help with this process.

```bash
cargo flash --chip <target_chip> --program
target/thumbv6m-none-
eabi/debug/your_project.uf2
```

5. **Debugging Embedded Code**: To debug embedded systems, you can use GDB (GNU Debugger). With the correct toolchain installed, you can debug your embedded code using GDB's remote debugging capabilities.

3. Using `probe-rs` for Debugging

`probe-rs` is a Rust-based debugging tool for embedded systems that provides a way to interact with microcontrollers, perform JTAG/SWD debugging, and load firmware onto devices. It's compatible with a wide range of microcontrollers, including ARM and RISC-V platforms.

For example, using `probe-rs`, you can connect to a microcontroller and perform debugging:

bash

```
cargo install probe-rs
probe-rs --chip <chip_name> debug
```

Real-Time Operating Systems (RTOS): How to Integrate Rust with RTOS for Performance-Critical Applications

Embedded systems often need to perform tasks within strict timing constraints. This is where **Real-Time Operating Systems (RTOS)** come into play. An RTOS is designed to handle real-time tasks where the system must respond to inputs within a guaranteed time frame. For example, in automotive systems, medical devices, or robotics, it's critical that operations occur in a predictable and timely manner.

1. What is an RTOS?

An RTOS is an operating system that supports real-time applications by managing hardware resources, scheduling tasks, and ensuring that high-priority tasks are executed within time constraints. Unlike general-purpose operating systems, RTOSs focus on predictable, low-latency task execution.

In embedded systems, there are typically two types of real-time systems:

- **Hard Real-Time Systems**: These systems must meet strict timing requirements, such as safety-critical applications.
- **Soft Real-Time Systems**: These systems have more lenient timing constraints, where missing a deadline occasionally is tolerable.

2. Integrating Rust with RTOS

Rust's performance and memory safety make it an ideal candidate for developing real-time systems. Although Rust does not yet have a full-fledged standard RTOS, there are libraries and tools that integrate Rust with existing RTOS environments, including:

- **FreeRTOS**: A popular, open-source RTOS that can be used with microcontrollers.
- **RTIC (Real-Time Interrupt-driven Concurrency)**: A framework designed specifically for embedded systems in Rust. RTIC allows you to build real-time, interrupt-driven systems with minimal overhead.

RTIC uses Rust's concurrency model, including its `async`/`await` syntax, to handle tasks concurrently while guaranteeing that each task meets its timing constraints.

3. Setting Up an RTOS in Rust

To set up an RTOS environment in Rust, we need to configure the system for interrupt handling, scheduling, and task prioritization. RTIC, in particular, offers a declarative model for building embedded applications with real-time guarantees.

Here's an example of using **RTIC** to manage a real-time task:

```toml
[dependencies]
rtic = "0.5"
cortex-m = "0.7"
cortex-m-rt = "0.7"
rust
```

```rust
#![no_std]
#![no_main]

use rtic::app;

#[app(device = stm32f4::stm32f407, peripherals =
true)]
const APP: () = {
    #[task]
    fn blink(c: blink::Context) {
        // This task runs with real-time guarantees
    }
```

```
};
```

In this code:

- We use RTIC's `#[app]` attribute to define an RTOS application with tasks that execute in response to hardware interrupts.
- The `blink` task is a simple example where the system guarantees that the task will run at a specified time, making it ideal for timing-sensitive operations like toggling LEDs.

Hands-on Project: Writing a Rust Program for a Basic Microcontroller, Like an Arduino

In this project, we'll write a basic embedded Rust program for an **Arduino** microcontroller. The goal is to control an LED connected to one of the pins of the Arduino using a simple Rust program.

1. Setting Up the Environment for Arduino

To develop for Arduino with Rust, we need to set up the Rust toolchain for cross-compilation. Follow these steps to get started:

1. **Install the ARM Target for Arduino**: Use the `rustup` tool to install the appropriate target for the Arduino platform. For example, for Arduino Uno (which uses the ATmega328P microcontroller), we can use the following command:

```
bash
```

```
rustup target add avr-atmega328p-none-gnu
```

2. **Install `avr-gcc` Toolchain**: You need to install the `avr-gcc` toolchain, which is used to compile code for AVR microcontrollers like the one used in Arduino. On Linux, you can install it using:

```
bash
```

```
sudo apt-get install avr-gcc
```

3. **Set Up the `Cargo.toml` for Arduino Development**: In your `Cargo.toml`, you'll need to add dependencies for embedded development:

```
toml
```

```
[dependencies]
avr-hal = "0.4"
```

The `avr-hal` crate provides hardware abstraction layers (HAL) for AVR microcontrollers, simplifying access to peripherals like GPIO pins, timers, and more.

2. Writing the LED Blinking Program

Now that the environment is set up, let's write a simple program to blink an LED on the Arduino. Here's an example of how to control an LED using the `avr-hal` crate:

```rust
#![no_std]
#![no_main]

use avr_hal_generic::prelude::*;
use avr_hal_generic::atmega328p::Peripherals;

#[panic_handler]
fn panic(_info: &core::panic::PanicInfo) -> ! {
    loop {}
}

#[no_mangle]
pub extern "C" fn main() -> ! {
    let dp = Peripherals::take().unwrap();
    let mut portb = dp.PORTB.split();
    let mut led = portb.pb5.into_output(&mut portb.ddr);

    loop {
        led.set_high(); // Turn LED on
        delay_ms(1000);
```

```
        led.set low(); // Turn LED off
        delay_ms(1000);
    }
}


fn delay_ms(ms: u16) {
    for _ in 0..ms {
        for _ in 0..1_000 {
            // Busy wait
        }
    }
}
```

In this example:

- We use the `avr-hal` crate to interact with the hardware on the Arduino.
- The program blinks an LED connected to pin 13 of the Arduino by toggling the state of the pin every second.
- We implement a simple `delay_ms` function using a busy-wait loop to create a delay, simulating a sleep function.

3. Compiling and Flashing the Program

After writing the program, we need to compile it for the target architecture and flash it to the microcontroller. You can use `cargo` to build the project:

```bash
bash
```

```bash
cargo build --target avr-atmega328p-none-gnu
```

Then, use `avrdude` (or a similar tool) to flash the compiled program to your Arduino:

```bash
bash
```

```bash
avrdude -c arduino -p m328p -P /dev/ttyUSB0 -U
flash:w:target/avr-atmega328p-none-
gnu/debug/your_program.hex
```

Replace `/dev/ttyUSB0` with the correct device path for your Arduino.

Conclusion

In this chapter, we've explored embedded systems programming with Rust. We've learned about setting up development environments for embedded Rust, handling low-level hardware interactions, and integrating Rust with real-time operating systems (RTOS) to build performance-critical applications. We also built a simple program to control an LED on an Arduino microcontroller, demonstrating the power of Rust for embedded development.

Rust's performance and memory safety guarantees make it an excellent choice for embedded systems, where hardware resources are limited, and reliability is crucial. By using tools like `cargo`, `probe-rs`, and libraries such as `rtic`, Rust allows developers to build embedded systems that are both efficient and robust, without sacrificing control over the hardware.

As you continue to explore embedded Rust, you'll discover more powerful tools and frameworks for building everything from simple microcontroller applications to complex real-time systems. Rust's growing ecosystem for embedded development is making it easier than ever to leverage its unique advantages in this space.

Chapter 15: Advanced Rust: Building Production-Ready Applications

Performance Optimization: Techniques for Optimizing Rust Programs for Speed and Memory Usage

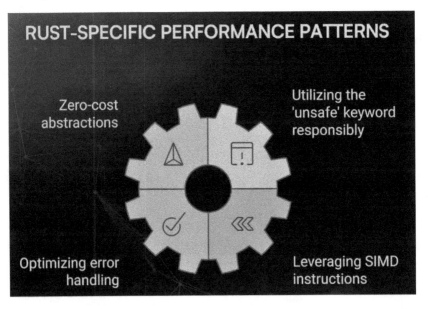

Rust is known for its performance—one of its core design principles is to offer near-C-like performance while maintaining memory safety. This makes Rust a powerful choice for systems-level programming, where every CPU cycle and byte of memory counts. However, writing high-performance Rust code isn't always automatic, and it requires some knowledge of best practices for performance optimization.

In this section, we'll discuss various techniques for optimizing Rust programs, both in terms of execution speed and memory usage. The strategies we cover will help ensure that your Rust applications run as efficiently as possible, which is particularly important in production-ready systems where performance is a critical factor.

1. Profiling Rust Code

Before diving into optimization techniques, it's crucial to understand where the bottlenecks in your code are. **Profiling** is the process of analyzing your program to identify performance bottlenecks. In Rust, profiling is done using external tools like `perf`, `valgrind`, or `cargo-bench`. These tools help you identify which parts of your code are consuming the most resources, so you can focus your optimization efforts where they are needed most.

- `cargo-bench`: This is a built-in tool that allows you to benchmark your Rust code by running specific benchmarks. You can annotate functions with `#[bench]` to create benchmarks, and `cargo bench` will execute them to measure performance.

- `perf`: A powerful tool for performance analysis, `perf` allows you to profile your program while it's running. It provides insights into CPU usage, cache misses, and function call counts.
- `valgrind`: Another tool that can help detect performance issues, including memory leaks, uninitialized memory, and inefficient memory usage.

2. Optimizing for Speed

Rust's ownership system inherently ensures that operations on data are safe, but in some cases, these safety checks can introduce performance overhead. Understanding how to write more efficient code in Rust while maintaining safety is key to building high-performance applications.

Here are some common techniques to optimize for speed:

- **Avoid Unnecessary Cloning**: In Rust, cloning data can be costly in terms of both time and memory. Instead of cloning data, consider passing references whenever possible. Rust's borrowing system ensures that data can be safely shared without the need for ing, as long as you don't need to mutate it.

  ```rust
  ```

```
let s = String::from("Hello, world!");
let slice = &s;  // No cloning, just a
reference
```

- **Minimize Heap Allocations**: Allocating memory on the heap is slower than working with stack-based data. Whenever possible, try to use stack-allocated data types like arrays, slices, and structs. If you need dynamic memory allocation, consider using efficient data structures like `VecDeque` or `BTreeMap`.

- **Leverage `unsafe` for Performance**: Rust's safety guarantees come with some overhead, especially when working with low-level system components. In performance-critical applications, you can use `unsafe` blocks to bypass certain safety checks, but use them sparingly. Always ensure that the safety requirements are met manually when using `unsafe`.

```rust
let x: i32 = unsafe { std::mem::transmute(42)
}; // Unsafe operation
```

- **Inlining Functions**: Inlining small functions can eliminate the overhead of function calls. Rust generally performs inlining automatically when possible, but you can also hint to the compiler that certain functions should be inlined using the `#[inline(always)]` attribute.

```rust
#[inline(always)]
fn fast_add(a: i32, b: i32) -> i32 {
    a + b
}
```

- **Using `std::mem::ManuallyDrop`**: In some situations, Rust's automatic memory management system might perform more work than necessary (e.g., double drop operations). You can use `std::mem::ManuallyDrop` to tell the compiler that certain data doesn't need to be dropped manually, which can optimize memory usage in specific situations.

3. Optimizing Memory Usage

Memory usage optimization is essential in embedded systems or any performance-critical application. In Rust, the ownership system prevents issues like double frees and memory leaks, but there are still ways to optimize how memory is used.

- **Minimize Memory Allocations**: Avoid unnecessary memory allocations, especially when working with large datasets.

Use data structures that allocate memory efficiently, such as `Vec` for dynamic arrays, `HashMap` for key-value pairs, or `String` for string manipulations.

- **Use `Box` for Heap Allocation**: If you need to allocate data on the heap, use `Box`, a heap-allocated smart pointer. The `Box` type provides efficient ownership and deallocation of heap memory.

```rust
let b = Box::new(42); // Efficient heap
allocation
```

- **Avoid Memory Fragmentation**: In long-running applications, memory fragmentation can cause performance issues. Rust's memory allocator is quite efficient, but it's still a good idea to be mindful of how you allocate and free memory, especially when dealing with many small allocations.
- **Zeroing Memory**: For security and performance reasons, zeroing out sensitive data from memory is often necessary. You can use `std::ptr::write_bytes` for low-level memory clearing operations.

4. Concurrent and Parallel Execution

Rust's concurrency model allows you to write safe, concurrent code that can execute on multiple CPU cores. Parallelism and concurrency are key to optimizing performance in multi-core systems.

- **Concurrency with `async/await`**: Asynchronous programming allows you to handle many I/O-bound tasks concurrently without blocking the execution of other tasks. By using `async/await`, you can write high-concurrency applications with minimal overhead.

- **Parallelism with Threads**: For CPU-bound tasks, parallelism is crucial. Rust provides powerful thread management through the `std::thread` module. Using threads effectively can help you utilize multi-core systems fully, but keep in mind that spawning too many threads or creating threads too frequently can be costly.

```rust

use std::thread;

fn compute() {
    let handle = thread::spawn(|| {
        // Expensive computation here
    });
    handle.join().unwrap();
}
```

Rust's FFI (Foreign Function Interface): Interfacing with C Libraries and Writing Bindings

Rust's Foreign Function Interface (FFI) allows you to call functions and use libraries written in other programming languages, especially C. This feature is crucial when you need to integrate with existing libraries or leverage hardware-specific functionality.

1. Understanding FFI in Rust

FFI in Rust is based on the `unsafe` keyword and allows direct interaction with external code. Rust provides a straightforward way to call C functions from Rust through the `extern` keyword.

Here's a basic example of how to call a C function from Rust:

1. **C Code** (`example.c`):

   ```c
   #include <stdio.h>

   void hello_world() {
       printf("Hello, World from C!\n");
   }
   ```

2. **Rust Code**:

```rust

extern "C" {
    fn hello_world();  // Declare the external
C function
}

fn main() {
    unsafe {
        hello_world();  // Call the C function
    }
}
```

In this code:

- We use `extern "C"` to declare a function that is written in C. This allows us to call `hello_world()` from Rust.
- The `unsafe` block is necessary because calling foreign code can break Rust's safety guarantees.

2. Using C Libraries in Rust

To use C libraries in Rust, you'll typically need to link the library during compilation. Rust provides the `bindgen` crate, which automatically generates Rust FFI bindings to C libraries. This is especially useful when dealing with large C libraries.

For example, to use a C library like `libm` (the math library), you would:

1. **Install the Library** (e.g., `libm`):
   o On Linux, you can install it using your package manager (e.g., `sudo apt-get install libm-dev`).
2. **Generate Bindings with `bindgen`:**
   o Install `bindgen` by adding it to your `Cargo.toml`:

   ```toml
   toml
   ```

   ```toml
   [build-dependencies]
   bindgen = "0.59"
   ```

   o Use `bindgen` to generate bindings:

   ```bash
   bash
   ```

   ```bash
   bindgen wrapper.h -o bindings.rs
   ```

   o The generated `bindings.rs` will allow you to use the C functions directly in Rust.

3. Example: Calling C's `malloc` and `free`

You can also call C functions for dynamic memory allocation, such as `malloc` and `free`:

```rust
rust

extern "C" {
    fn malloc(size: usize) -> *mut u8;
    fn free(ptr: *mut u8);
}

fn main() {
    unsafe {
        let ptr = malloc(10);
        if !ptr.is_null() {
            // Use the allocated memory
            free(ptr);
        }
    }
}
```

In this example:

- We declare C functions `malloc` and `free` for memory allocation and deallocation.
- The `unsafe` block is required because dereferencing raw pointers and calling foreign functions are inherently unsafe operations in Rust.

Security Considerations: Writing Secure Code and Avoiding Common Pitfalls

Rust's focus on memory safety inherently prevents many common programming mistakes that lead to security vulnerabilities, such as buffer overflows, use-after-free errors, and data races. However, writing secure code still requires an understanding of potential pitfalls and best practices to ensure that your application is resilient against attacks.

1. Handling Untrusted Input Safely

When dealing with user input or data from external sources (such as files or network requests), it's essential to validate and sanitize that input before processing it. Rust's type system helps prevent some issues by ensuring that data is correctly typed and checked at compile time.

- **Avoid Buffer Overflows**: Rust's memory safety features ensure that array bounds and buffer accesses are checked, which prevents buffer overflow attacks.

- **Use the Standard Library Safely**: Rust's standard library offers functions like `std::str::from_utf8()` and `std::fs::File::open()` that properly handle errors and ensure safe handling of untrusted data.

2. Secure Memory Handling

Although Rust's ownership and borrowing system prevent common memory-related errors, you still need to be mindful of unsafe code, especially when interacting with low-level APIs, external libraries, or manually handling memory.

- **Avoid Use of `unsafe` Unless Necessary**: `unsafe` bypasses Rust's safety guarantees, so it should be used sparingly and only when you have carefully verified that the operation is safe.
- **Prevent Data Races**: Rust's concurrency model ensures that data cannot be simultaneously accessed and modified by multiple threads unless explicitly handled. However, you should still be mindful of thread safety when working with shared resources.

3. Cryptography and Secure Communication

For applications requiring cryptography (e.g., secure communications or password hashing), Rust provides libraries like `rust-openssl`, `ring`, and `sodiumoxide`. These libraries allow you to implement secure communication channels and protect sensitive data. When using cryptographic functions, ensure that they are implemented correctly and securely.

Hands-on Project: Develop a Real-Time System That Integrates Rust with a C Library, Optimized for Performance

In this project, we'll develop a real-time system that interacts with a C library for optimized performance. We will integrate Rust with a C library (e.g., a C-based sensor library) and optimize the application for real-time performance. Our goal is to demonstrate the combination of Rust's memory safety with the speed and efficiency of C libraries.

1. Setting Up the Project

Start by creating a new Rust project:

bash

```
cargo new rust_c_integration --bin
cd rust_c_integration
```

2. Linking with a C Library

We will integrate a simple C library that interacts with a sensor. Write a simple C library for reading sensor data:

c

```
// sensor.c
```

```c
#include <stdio.h>

int read_sensor_data() {
    // Simulating sensor reading
    return 42;
}
```

Compile this into a shared library:

bash

```bash
gcc -shared -o libsensor.so sensor.c
```

3. Creating Rust Bindings

Use `bindgen` to generate bindings for the C library:

bash

```bash
bindgen wrapper.h -o src/bindings.rs
```

4. Calling the C Library in Rust

Now, write the Rust code to call the C library's function:

rust

```rust
extern crate libc;

extern "C" {
    fn read_sensor_data() -> i32;
}
```

```
fn main() {
    unsafe {
        let data = read_sensor_data();
        println!("Sensor Data: {}", data);
    }
}
```

5. Running the Application

Build and run the application:

```bash
cargo build
cargo run
```

This will call the `read_sensor_data` function from the C library and display the sensor data in the Rust application.

Conclusion

In this chapter, we explored several advanced topics that are critical for building production-ready Rust applications. We learned how to optimize Rust programs for speed and memory usage, interface with C libraries using Rust's FFI, and ensure that our code is secure. The hands-on project demonstrated how to integrate Rust with a C library for optimized real-time performance, showing how Rust can be used in performance-critical applications.

Rust's low-level control, combined with its strong safety guarantees, makes it an excellent choice for systems programming, and by leveraging advanced optimization, FFI, and security practices, you can build robust, high-performance applications for a wide range of use cases.